CHRYSALIS

CHRYSALIS

From Corporate Executive to Intuitive Artist
A Spiritual Adventure

KATHY FORD

Printed in the United States of America
Published in Hellertown, PA
Cover design by Anna Magruder
Images by Kathy Ford
Library of Congress Control Number 2025911885
ISBN 979-8-89420-055-2
For more information or to place bulk orders, contact the author or publisher at Jennifer@BrightCommunications.net.

Bright
COMMUNICATIONS

To my sister Sue, for starting me on this journey

Contents

Introduction

And then it happened. A lifequake, I called it, initiated by an unexpected downsizing, which shook me out of my complacency and turned my life upside down. Every aspect of my life—literally everything I believed, valued, or owned—ultimately fell away, left, or changed. I was liquified, like a caterpillar, and held in my own personal chrysalis.

When I emerged years later, my life was as completely transformed as the caterpillar's, that lowly leaf munching twig crawler, who miraculously becomes an airborne nectar-sipping butterfly.

I thought a lot about the process of the caterpillar's metamorphosis. Did you know that caterpillars have specialized cells called imaginal cells that hold the DNA blueprint for the butterfly-to-be? The imaginal cells remain dormant until the chrysalis is formed, and then they awaken and begin to multiply.

The caterpillar's immune system, however, perceives them as alien, not-self, because they are so different, and proceeds to kill them off. Eventually, though, the imaginal cells win the war. The caterpillar's body breaks down into a liquified goo, and the to-be butterfly's body begins to develop.

I've often wondered what entices a caterpillar to climb up that last twig, hang upside down, and wrap itself in its own personal sleeping bag. What motivates it to voluntarily release its old life completely and allow its liquified body, its essence, to be held inside that fragile chrysalis?

Yet only then, in that state of complete surrender and utter vulnerability, can transformation happen. After what must feel like a lifetime to that little being, it finally breaks free of its self-imposed prison, miraculously emerging as a butterfly.

Based on what happened in my life, I firmly believe that imaginal cells exist in humans too. At least they did in me. There must have been a blueprint for what, or who, I was supposed to become, but like the caterpillar, I was unaware of it. I was nudged down an unexpected path to transformation, just like the caterpillar was moved to climb that last twig.

———

I spent many years as a caterpillar, focused on living a good, prosperous, suburban life—eating tasty leaves, growing bigger and stronger. It was a good life with interesting and challenging work, a good home life, great husband and kids, close to parents and siblings. Interesting vacations, digging for dinosaur bones in Montana, sitting atop the Acropolis, driving Vespas through Rome, kayaking in Belize. Life was good. Very good.

Occasionally, though, a question, *Is this all there is?* would niggle at me, accompanied by a vague restlessness. What was missing? I had it all! Still, I ignored the question for years, snuffing it out and distracting myself with busyness and climbing the corporate ladder, setting my sights on the socially acceptable goals of position, power, and prestige.

At some point, though, after my kids were off to college, and I had reached the upper rungs of the proverbial corporate ladder more than once, the restlessness became a yearning that gnawed at me. Some part of me, my imaginal cells I guess, seemed to know that there was supposed to be more to my life than monthly results and office politics. A life I couldn't imagine kept nudging me, and even though I was becoming increasingly dissatisfied, I clung to the life I knew. Immune cells 10, Imaginal cells 0.

At the time, I had no idea that my life was already starting to undergo a complete transformation. I thought I would be quickly past the unexpected and uncomfortable life transition caused by the downsizing. A few weeks, a month, six months tops. Typical type-A me was impatient to be on my way to whatever came next. Little did I know it would take seven long years until I would emerge from my chrysalis.

Many people have spent time in the chrysalis, which is more commonly known as the Dark Night of the Soul. I choose not to use that term, however, because it emphasizes the heart-wrenching aspects of this time. Don't get me wrong, there were many heart-wrenching, terrifying times. And although my time in the chrysalis often felt like a punishment, I couldn't see until much later that it truly was one of the greatest gifts of my life.

More importantly, there were many other gifts waiting to be discovered there, in my chrysalis. Gifts of personal growth and insight were offered through the remarkable experiences I had during those years. They were gifts that, in hindsight, I could not have received any other way.

During those years, my type-A tendency frequently raised its impatient head. I heard the message, over and over, "Opening the chrysalis too soon kills the butterfly. The journey takes what it takes." I understood. I didn't like it but understood. The last thing I wanted was to be spilled out into the world as a puddle of goo.

I think caterpillars get impatient too. I once saw one, wiggling and twisting within its chrysalis, imagining its little voice crying, "GET ME OUTTA HERE!" I could definitely relate. The time I spent in my chrysalis felt endless, mostly because I had no idea how long it would last. I struggled with hopelessness, anger, and frustration because nothing I tried to do to hurry the process along worked. Not one thing.

Breaking free of my chrysalis marked the end of this remarkable phase of my life—and the start of a new one. I can tell you that the struggles and the lessons didn't end there, but by then I realized that they never would. But they *would* change, and apparently, I was ready to tackle them.

This is the story of the adventures, awakenings, and challenges that I experienced during my time in my chrysalis—my transition from intense corporate executive to spiritual seeker and artist.

I am grateful to all the amazing teachers, both physical and non-physical, who showed up and lovingly guided my way. I am also grateful to my extraordinary circle of friends, who encouraged me to explore and experience new aspects of life and who accepted me, no matter what.

Finally, I am grateful to my younger self, for her courage, curiosity, and stubbornness and for keeping such good notes! Her observations of our experiences have added accuracy, depth, and detail to these pages.

Chapter 1: Angels

I was at the top of my game career-wise—Vice President of Marketing in a consumer products company. I drove a company car and was paid a great salary with a substantial bonus riding on delivering results.

It was a tough assignment though. The toughest I'd tackled. The company was in bad shape, battling poor financial performance, lack of innovation or market leadership, and outdated manufacturing facilities. I was part of an entirely new management team assigned to turn things around, to bring new life, energy, direction, and profitability to that very unhealthy business.

For two years, we worked hard to reinvigorate the product lines with on-trend designs, sharp pricing, improved quality, and on-time deliveries. It was a huge challenge though because the major retailers who were our largest customers were starting to source similar products from China at significantly lower cost. Even more distressing, we learned that they were taking our proprietary product designs to China to be manufactured—without permission. We lost sales because of this, which reduced production in our factories and exacerbated the company's financial challenges.

Amidst all the daily drama and stress, my sister gifted me an "angel" reading for my birthday. I should explain that my sister, who is a few years older than me, had been searching for meaning in her life, and she found it, at least in part, in what I called the "woo-woo world" of metaphysics and angels. For years, I quietly scoffed at her, thinking that she was a bit "out there."

She and I were philosophically light-years apart. I was all about how much money I could make, how big a title I could earn, and how much power I could wield at work. My life revolved around meetings and deadlines. I had no time for spiritual contemplation.

So for her to give me an angel reading made total sense to her, but it certainly wasn't anything I'd ever considered having or needing. I thought it was about as useful a gift as receiving two left shoes that also happened to be two sizes too small. Still, I wondered, *What exactly is an angel reading and what would I even do with it?* Sometimes we get exactly what we need, even if it's not what we want. The angel reading turned out to be that for me. I didn't realize it at the time, in fact not for a long time, but it was the first of a series of events that completely changed my life.

Well, I thought, *what the heck.* My life had become less than ideal. The stress at work was chronic and intense, and I was getting worn out. *Maybe I'll learn something useful.*

Uncharacteristically, I took the day of my angel reading off, made time to just be quiet, even did a few yoga stretches. That was all very unlike me, but it seemed a respectful way to prepare to speak with angels, if that was indeed what was going to happen. I even wrote down some questions I might ask this angel person. Still, I was understandably skeptical about the whole thing.

When the appointed time came, I called the number. I spoke with a nice woman named Connie, who explained that during this session she would "get out of the way," and the angels would speak to me directly through her.

She explained that angels are typically groups of beings who work together, sort of like a cloud of consciousness. To simplify communication with humans, they speak in one voice. The entity Abraham, channeled by Esther Hicks, is also a group entity speaking with one voice, and so is Kryon, who is channeled by Lee Caroll.

Connie went on to explain that I could ask questions, or I could request that they tell me about my "sacred wheel," which would provide information about thirteen important aspects of my life, such as how I communicate, what my talents are, and the status of my relationships. She said the angels like to use animals to represent the essence of each aspect and then explain what they mean.

My strategy at work had always been to get others to speak first in meetings so I could gauge where they were coming from and then formulate my position and responses from there. Applying the same strategy with the angel reading, I opted for the sacred wheel to avoid giving this person information that she might use to make up advice for me.

What happened next was a complete surprise. After a brief pause (I assumed she was "getting out of the way"), Connie started speaking. Fast. I struggled to keep up as I took notes. She never paused for more than a quick breath. For nearly an hour, she described each aspect of my life, offering insights and suggestions for growth in each one.

The weird thing was that she was dead on. It was like she knew me from the inside out, and I didn't know her from Adam. Later, I asked my sister how much she had told this lady about me, and she said nothing—only that I was her sister. I was flabbergasted. How could anyone do what Connie just did? If it was fake, she would have had to pause and think up more stuff, or if she had planned it out in advance, how could she have been so right on target? The angels also said some surprising things too—things that didn't make a lot of sense at that moment in my life but I wondered if maybe they would in the future.

For example, my health and work were symbolized as a turtle. I had everything inside me to heal myself. I use the turtle's protective shell to keep myself safe. (It's true I was generally healthy and had learned to protect myself from the negativity and politicking at work.) Regarding work, the angels said I had the tendency to take on entire jobs without delegating, suggesting that I let others help and take on responsibilities. (Also, too true!)

The raccoon symbolized the way I communicate, which chatters a lot when excited. (Like me, when I am excited. But when I'm not enthused or engaged, I am generally very quiet.) Referring to the mask and coloring of the raccoon, the angels said that I see the black and the white (both sides) in situations but also the shades of grey, enabling me to communicate in neutrality. (True ... most of the time.)

Physical abundance was symbolized by the giraffe, which represented great abundance. But like the giraffe, which has ungraceful movements, abundance would come to me in spurts, in an uneven pattern. The angels said I couldn't plan abundance, but they suggested that I "stay in the flow" and trust myself, stay aware of what patterns were working and follow them. (This didn't make much sense at the time because I was doing well financially, with a healthy savings account. But looking back years later, this ended up being a helpful bit of advice.)

Regarding how comfortable I felt in the world, the black swan was the symbol, indicating a strong soul connection to Australia, New Zealand, and Tasmania. The angels said this was an unusual, unique symbol and suggested that I visualize a black swan gliding on a pond to discover why there is so much connection to that part of the world. This did not make much sense to me at that time, and the visualization I attempted didn't unveil any new information. I filed it away as a curiosity, maybe something to think about later.

The angels also told me that an angel named George was working with me and had already made his presence known. I hadn't made the connection until they told me. He kept pushing a spot in the middle of my forehead, and I felt it. Literally like someone was pushing a button, about an inch above the top of my nose. It was distracting and a bit annoying as I tried to focus on whatever I was working on. I kept rubbing the spot to get it to stop feeling tingly.

My sister told me that the spot was my "third eye" and recommended I get an audio series called "Energy Anatomy" by Carolyn Myss. I listened to it while driving back and forth to work. I found it to be full of fascinating information about each of the body's chakras, including how memories and emotions are stored in these various parts of the body. For example, the third eye is associated with intuition. George was apparently poking this spot to awaken my intuition.

After the angel reading was over, I had pages of notes. I'd never had an experience like that, and it made me curious about those angels. Do they really, actively participate in our lives? Do they regularly interact with people like me as though they are friends or teachers?

Then I vividly recalled a memory from my childhood. I was probably three or four years old.

I was lying on the grass in the front yard of my house, noticing how the clouds moved across the sky—bunching, breaking apart, racing, joining others, or disappearing into nothingness, as ever-changing and restless as the ocean. With the ocean's same moods. Wild storminess and placid flow. That day, they were playful.

In quiet moments like that, when there were no distractions like TV or people talking, I noticed another presence with me. A consciousness that was not my own. With me, but not me.

The "presence" felt different—intelligent, with good intent and a personal interest in me. Different from a human presence. Bigger, purer, clearer. Distinct. Sometimes more than one "presence" kept me company.

I thought of them as my invisible friends. Because they were. They were my friends, and they were invisible. At three or four years old, it didn't seem odd. Everyone had invisible friends, didn't they?

These friends knew me so well, better than I knew myself. Like they had known me forever and were a part of me. Like the beating of my heart, which I also only noticed in those quiet moments.

I felt completely loved by them, always. They didn't have specific names or personalities. They were just a group of friends who hung out with me, especially when I was by myself and quiet. They just happened to be invisible. Our conversations took place within my mind, although I wouldn't swear that I didn't sometimes answer them out loud.

That day, I turned over onto my belly and watched the ants go about their busy day. One climbed up a stalk of grass and then went down again. Others stayed at ground level, weaving around all the obstacles to get to their destination. My mind was wide open and curious.

What do you think they think about? a quiet voice asked inside my head.

Ah, there were my friends, being curious *with* me.

They asked simple questions or made observations about the world around me. They nudged me to think wider, to think about things most kids maybe don't think about, like, if ants think, what do they think about? That's a lot of thinking. My friends encouraged my natural curiosity, and they helped me appreciate the other lives around me, like ants and trees and even skunk cabbage.

———

The angel reading fired up a similar curiosity in me, all those years later. I was fascinated by the messages given during the reading. I very much wanted to learn more from them, but I had no idea how to go about it.

The internet, still in its infancy in those days, turned out to be a wonderful source of information—like Magic Mirror from *Snow White*. Have a question? Ask Magic Mirror, and you'll get an answer. And that answer often led to more questions and more answers. The library of the world was at my fingertips, and through it I found out a lot about angels.

I became aware of a whole subculture of people who work with angels—angel therapists, angel oracle card readers, and other angel channelers. "Fascinating," as Spock would say. And like Spock, my logical mind assessed it all with a healthy mix of skepticism and curiosity. Well, there was nothing like direct experience to decide for myself.

I had learned from Magic Mirror that repeating numbers were one way the angels used to let us know they were nearby. Son of a gun, *I had* been noticing repeating numbers showing up everywhere. Every time I glanced at a clock, it would say 3:33 or 4:44 or 1:11 in an oddly frequent regularity. I noticed license plate numbers too. I'd see ANGL-111, or LUV-444. I had never paid much attention to license plates before, except to play the "state" game on road trips as a kid.

The repetition of numbers, everywhere I looked, was weird and intriguing. It couldn't be just random occurrences. There were too many of them! I imagined that the angels were numerically shouting at me. I had a funny mental picture of several angels, holding signs with numbers on them, jumping up and down, waving the signs, running around me, generally trying to get my attention. Apparently, angels have a sense of humor.

I also began to notice other things, such as a song playing on the radio with just the words I needed to hear. Or I'd read a book or watch a movie with exactly the information or perspective that I needed in that moment.

I could only surmise from these coincidences that angels actually *did* want to communicate with me. It was a working theory anyway, and it was a start. Now, how should I go about opening up a direct line of communication? How would I talk with them, and then hear what they had to say?

I started making a little quiet time in my days. It seemed a respectful thing to do to acknowledge the unique opportunity that seemed to be presenting itself to me. I made some time for the chance to get to know other angels, who were willing (wanting?) to work with me from the unseen realms.

I'm not going to lie. It didn't go well at first. I never was much good at quieting my mind. I tried focusing on my breathing but fell asleep instead. I tried staring at a candle flame, but my mind wandered all over the place.

The books I read on how to meditate didn't help me either. I fell asleep every time. That was great if I wanted some rest, but my quest was for a new, different kind of communication, a conversation with angels. I had to find a different way in.

The more I tried to stop my chittering, mundane thoughts, the more I got distracted with the act of stopping them. Eventually, I imagined those thoughts as a river and simply allowed it to flow. I mentally moved away from the river, turning my attention elsewhere, and I finally found a path into deeper, quieter, inner waters. This actually worked. I could allow the river of thoughts to flow, over there, and focus on what was going on here, inside.

Eventually, I found that keeping a journal and pen with me worked even better to help me stay focused. I sat cross-legged on the sofa, cup of coffee or tea nearby, journal in my lap, pen in my hand, poised to write. Sometimes I lit a candle to sanctify the moment. I slowed and deepened my breathing deliberately, in the way of yoga. Slow breath in, slow breath out. Notice the breath. In, pause, and out, pause. In, and out. Slowing down. My thoughts entrained to this rhythm, quieting, relaxing.

The river of thoughts still flowed, but I just let them go without trying to eliminate them. They were the mundane, scurrying thoughts that endlessly flitted around all day long—items for the grocery list, people I wanted to call, on and on, endless mind chatter. Amazing, really, in a sad sort of way. Imagine what would happen if I could fill my head with deep, questioning, meaningful thoughts instead.

Finally, with my mind quiet, I imagined that I was in an empty room with speakers on the wall. I invited communication, then waited, listening. Sometimes, especially at first, I received nothing at all.

Since George had been the first angel to reach out to me, I decided he would be the first one I would try to contact on my own. I breathed, relaxed. In, and out, waiting for something different. And then it came. A phrase, a comment out of context with the rest of my thoughts. Like someone was actually talking to me in a conversational voice, except there was nothing to hear, no one to see. I wrote each comment down as it came and waited again. Bit by bit, a statement emerged.

> *You are so wound up all the time. We want you to find joy in each day. You are always striving and never stopping to enjoy the now. We are happy that you want to get to know us, but you can't do it all in one day! Relax and let us help.*
>
> *All will unfold as it is meant to. Some things could not have happened before now, and it is not yet time for other things. So again, relax and know that your transition has started, as planned before you were born.*
>
> *Remember to breathe deeply. We are with you. Be joyful as often as you can. Be grateful for all the wonderful gifts and people that surround you. Be an angel when you can. The rest will unfold. Get out in nature as often as you can. Take notes of our conversations. When you look back, you will be amazed at how things unfolded for you.*

He also told me that "they" were the same angels who were my childhood invisible friends. So, who *were* these guys anyway? Angels? Guardian angels? Archangels? Guides? Soul? Yes. No. Maybe. I didn't really know. I just knew they were supportive of me, interested in talking with me, and I was very grateful for that. Grateful that they had made themselves known to me when I was really young and apparently had stayed with me through all my life's ups and downs. True and forever friends, no matter what.

I found George to be very approachable, and his personality felt somehow familiar. He told me that in other circumstances (lifetimes) we worked together. An old and dear friend, then. This time around, we apparently were still working together, except that he stayed on the other side to better help me. He was playing the role of angel guide, and I was apparently playing the role of human angel. Which we all are, I was told. We are all angels who have come to Earth to learn, to expand our wisdom through physical experience, and help when we can.

I told him that I thought George was a rather mundane name for an angel. He "laughed" and said that it just happened to be the name he was using at the moment, that angelic names are used for us humans so we can relate to them. Where he was, on the other side, a soul's individual vibration was all that was ever needed to recognize it. Each vibration is completely unique, like a thumbprint, and reflects the accumulated experiences and wisdom gained. Because of this, our vibrations evolve as we evolve as souls, but they still remain unmistakably and recognizably our own.

During my next conversation with George, he asked me to discipline my mind and stay present mentally when meditating.

———

I visualized us sitting on a park bench under a tree, looking out over a little lake. I was uncertain what was expected of me. I tried asking George a little bit about himself, you know, some small talk to break the ice. Nope. Nada. Silence. Sigh. I waited for ... I didn't know what. We sat side by side in silence for a long time. My mind slipped down its usual trivial bunny trails. I realized this and kept returning to the bench, waiting. Fidgeting. Pulling my sleeves down over my wrists, pulling my collar up tighter around my neck, the coolness of morning seeping into my outside physical body.

Eventually, I began to sink into an open receptive meditative state. Then music started playing in my head—the kind that goes round and round for days. I did my best to ignore it and focused on expanding the sense of peace that was beginning to emerge within me. George said,

Very good. You know, it's hard to communicate with all that mental chatter. Like being in a restaurant with loud music and lots of side conversation at the nearby tables. You hate that. I dislike it as well. So, when we're together, let's try to be in a quiet state so we can really talk without all the effort.

I liked this guy. He made sense.

Notice. I was already noticing. In this quiet inner space, I felt so solid inside. Grounded. Strong energetically. Present. Not scattered in the past or future. Here, solidly. My body's core felt like a cylinder, strangely like a large, vertical toilet paper roll, strong yet squishy and flexible but not hollow inside. Solid, golden, like bee's wax. Full.

———

Over time, I gained some proficiency at accessing the quiet place inside me. I started to discern different angelic personalities, each of them seeming to want to "have a chat" with me. At times, it was overwhelming. Eventually, we agreed on meeting and working with just a handful of these new friends at a time. Some became "regulars," and others stopped by for a chat only once or twice.

Slowly, I began to receive more information. Sometimes, it was a thought or concept that was out of context with the other mind chatter. Other times, it was an image or short mental "video". I learned to pause, rise out of the deep state I was in for a few moments, write it down, and then sink back down to listen again. This kept me focused on the conversation.

To my dismay, I discovered that the angels liked getting me up at 2, 3, or 4 am. Apparently, early morning was the best time for them to communicate, when my mental activity was at its lowest point after a night of rest. The stress of the previous day had been processed and released, and my mind was quiet and most receptive. Initially, I resisted this intrusion to my precious sleep time, rolling over and shutting my eyes tight. But they were quite persistent, and I ended up being wide awake and completely unable to fall back asleep anyway.

One early morning, I hit snooze on the 4 am alarm on my clock because I was still really sleepy. The second alarm I turned off. A few minutes later, I became aware that George was talking to me, saying,

First lesson: Show up for your life.

In other words, this morning time was the most important slice of the day. Don't waste it in a snooze.

Finally, we reached an accord. If I would willingly get out of bed and have a "chat," they promised that I would never be tired later in the day, regardless of how early I got up or how busy I would be. And truly, they kept their word. Not once was I tired after a pre-dawn conversation.

As I began reacquainting myself with these invisible angel friends, I noticed that their feel had changed a bit since my childhood days. But to be fair, so had I. I had become hardened, sarcastic, and interestingly, so had they, Whipping out a smart-ass comment from time to time to get my attention. And it worked.

For example, one day I was wallowing in self-pity at the unfairness of life and whining about it to them. Instead of the coddling, comforting response I had hoped to get, I heard,

> *Pull up your big girl panties and get on with your life!*

Whoa. What? Okay then. Geez! But that turned out to be exactly what I needed to hear. They had to get my attention to pull me out of my self-centered doldrums. Well, it worked! They loved me enough to figuratively smack me upside the head.

It also removed all doubt that I might have been just talking to myself and making up these inner dialogues. When I received a message and my reaction was, "What? You've *got* to be kidding!" That's when I knew for sure, *for sure,* that the message came from beyond myself.

———

The angels told me that profound healing can occur during a guided meditation. Connie had taught me a visualization called the "White Mountain," where one could speak soul-to-soul with another person. It was a useful tool for having a conversation with someone you were at odds with, whether living or already passed, for the purpose of reconciliation.

The general structure of the meditation was always the same, but the details within the imagery would change of their own accord with each visit, and the angels said the changes were not random. There was a reason that certain things changed, and by noticing and reflecting on what was different, I could glean more insight.

In preparation for my first trip to the Mountain, I needed to clarify both who I wanted to meet and what my goals were for the meeting. If I was going there to prove that I was right about something, to tell them off, or try to get the other person to accept my way of thinking, it was not appropriate to go. The meditation was not to be used in those ways.

Rather, it was an opportunity to say the things that were in my heart, which in normal life would be difficult or impossible to say to the other person. In return, I might receive a response, have a conversation, and possibly come to an agreement, a resolution, a healing for both parties.

The implications of this meditation were staggering. Imagine being able to come to peace with someone who died before an emotional hurt could be healed. Or being able to talk with the soul of an estranged friend to let them know how much you loved them.

The angels made it clear that the intent for a journey to the mountain must always be based in love and a desire for reconciliation. Results of a White Mountain conversation would usually be noticeable within a few days by a shift in attitude or circumstance. Sometimes the changes were subtle; sometimes they were life changing.

Following is a general description of a typical White Mountain experience and examples of how the details might change—in case you'd like to go. Keep in mind that this is how I experienced the meditation. It could be very different for you.

I slow my breath and calm my mind, then visualize the Mountain in the distance, its top covered in snow. A forest of trees flank its base. As I walk toward it, I find a path that winds its way back and forth up to the summit. Sometimes it is a very long path; sometimes it is much shorter or steeper. Sometimes it is easy to walk; sometimes it is rough and rocky.

I stop along the way, sitting by a babbling brook or watching a butterfly. Each journey to the top is different and an important part of preparing for the upcoming meeting. It cannot be rushed. There are gifts of insight or peace that can only be found on this upward trek to the summit. It is important to pay attention to what is seen, heard, or felt on the way up.

At the top, the first thing I notice is a lake. Sometimes it's a small pond. I take some time to look around and notice what else is there. One time the summit might be a wide-open field. Another time there might be a stand of trees, a single apple tree full of ripe apples, or a hut. The seasons can change there as well—a warm summer's day or a heavy snowstorm, for example.

On either side of the water is a bench. I sit on one and call the name of the person I wish to meet into the water. The person comes and sits on the other bench. Often the person called will appear in another form, like a frog or a bear. Or a large woman in skimpy clothes, lounging on a red velvet couch, munching grapes! It can be surprising!

As I reflect on how the person shows up, I learn a bit more about them. The form they choose to come in is important. If I look down at myself, I may see that I have shown up as something other than I expected too!

The conversation goes however it needs to— short or long, whispers, shouts, or images shared. And when all has been said and shared, the meditation ends—differently each time.

Meeting someone on the Mountain is sacred and powerful and is appropriate if true heart-felt reconciliation or forgiveness is the goal.

Chapter 2: Toppled

Getting to know the angels was a nice balance to the hectic days at work. And then one day, the corporate office made a surprise announcement that our division was going to be consolidating with another to cut costs. Our entire management team was let go. I was toppled from being relevant, important even, to extraneous in one conversation.

I was the lucky one, I suppose. The rest of the management team was asked to leave right away. I was required to stay on for three months to train the new team in order to receive a quite generous severance package, which would continue my VP income for six months. Plenty of time to find a new job.

Over the course of those first two months, information was transferred, and the new staff trained. This was accomplished well before my end date, and they were off and running. However, I was still required to go to the office every day for the third, very long, month. No one stopped by to ask a question—or even to visit. I was a *persona non grata*. Invisible. Alone, in my big office, my success "crumbled" all around me, laughing at me.

Being squeezed out of a very lucrative job was traumatic. My identity, sense of self-worth, and ego were all downsized too. It was a very strange and disorienting time.

In those last weeks at work, I was asked to run a meeting to review the new product ideas we had come up with for the coming year. I should mention here that there was no love lost between the sales team and me. They had consistently underdelivered on their promised revenue opportunities, and when the sales did not materialize, the warehouse bulged with the unsold products, making the company's cash flow problems worse. I was furious; they didn't care in the least.

I was not looking forward to this meeting, not at all. I had a heart full of hate and anger toward the sales team and struggled to get my feelings under control. I tried to detach myself from those emotions, but it was not easy. In fact, I didn't do a very good job of it at all. From my journal:

> *I've been preparing for the meeting. I thought I could escape without having to deal with the sales team again, but the entire sales team will be there.*
>
> *How can I get to the point where I am so detached that they mean no more to me than this pen I am writing with? Why do they bother me so much?*
>
> *I had a vision of where this business could go. It tallied with trend information from all over. The strategy was right, but I am viewed as incompetent. So not fair!*
>
> *Now not only do I have to present to these guys, but my successors will also be there. I have to face this and resolve it. I have so much hate for these guys. How do I let it go?*

The angels suggested that I forgive everyone at work who I thought was a problem. (Another "You've *got* to be kidding!" moment.) They said I needed to sever the negative cords tying me to that place so I could move on. Ugh, okay. I'll give it a go. In my mind, I bathed the buildings and everyone in them with a strong light as a blessing, and one by one I let them go, watching them float away into the bright light.

When the time to meet finally arrived, I thought I had gotten myself to the point where those guys were like pens to me—ready to be balanced, neutral, and non-engaged.

Five minutes before the meeting though, it felt like someone kicked or knifed me in my right kidney. I was in such pain. I couldn't stand, and I couldn't sit. I got bad cramps, hot flashes, chills. I felt like I was going to throw up and then faint. Then it started all over again.

Through all that, I tried to run the meeting. While I expected some battles, what happened was war. The sales team attacked every single concept we had come up with. The designs weren't good enough for them. They asked, What assurances could I give them that these trends would be right for the next year? Not enough designs. Pricing not sharp enough. It was an all-out attack.

Through it all, my body just fell apart. I barely made it home. I felt terrible. I threw up and went to bed. It was the lowest I'd felt in a long time—like a total failure. Even my body betrayed me. After all the work I did internally to prepare for that meeting, I couldn't see it through.

I wish I understood why it happened. I was already out the door. I didn't need this humiliation. I asked God to give me the strength and patience to finish my time. If nothing else, the job now smelled like a rotting corpse, instead of a newly departed lover. I just wanted to get away from it as soon as possible!

I reflected on what happened for quite a while. I tried to make some sense of it, to find some lesson I could grasp onto. Finally, it came to me that I had experienced *hate* in its raw state. Worse, that's what I had been sending to them, and I got it back with both barrels!

You reap what you sow. You receive what you give. Karma, baby. Wow. Tough lesson, but effective. The power of personal energy. I saw the shadow side of it that day. I could only assume, and hope, that the reverse also existed.

A few weeks later, I was asked to attend an offsite strategy meeting. It was my last obligation before leaving for good. It was hard to sit and listen to how terribly we (the previous management team) had messed things up, how we had no usable design or trend concepts. I felt so many overlapping, overwhelming feelings: embarrassment, sadness, disappointment, failure.

But I was not the only target. The new guys had also concluded that the manufacturing plants were in total disarray. Clearly the company could not make good products in the USA anymore, and also logistics had forgotten how to ship, schedule, and order material.

One good thing that came out of the meeting was that while I had felt sad at the thought of leaving, I now felt only relief that I didn't have to fight these battles anymore. Several times, as I listened to them talk, I thought to myself, *Who cares? How could anyone get so passionate about a broken business?* (Of course, that was me not so very long ago!) Everything about the company was turning into that pen after all. Just didn't matter anymore.

In hindsight, losing my job was the biggest gift I ever received. It didn't feel like it at the time. But the events of those last months left such a bad taste in my mouth that they compelled me to leave the corporate world firmly in the wake of my life and look for something different, very different. But what?

Chapter 3: Getting My Bearings

When I was finally free of my three-month work sentence, my husband and I took a trip to New Zealand. Traveling to the other side of the planet was the perfect way to get as far away from my old life as I possibly could! But first we attended the college graduation of our oldest son.

At the same time as our trip, our younger son was unexpectedly called up from the Marine Reserves for his first active tour of duty—to Kuwait. It was hard to watch him suspend his college studies, to take that path, to journey into war, to support his decisions. It was harder still because it was a challenge to talk with him. We were halfway around the world, and he was on the move too, from Ohio to California, then Germany and finally Kuwait.

The trip to New Zealand was truly a blessing. My husband and I had decided not to pre-plan the itinerary too much, but rather go with the flow. For me, the type-A planner, this was a challenge, but I hoped it would be a fun, freewheeling experience. We had set our sights on circumnavigating the South Island. Tales of its immense natural beauty made us want to see it all. The "soft" plan was to fly into Auckland (on the North Island), then head south, and fly back from Auckland again two weeks later.

However, once we got there, we were strongly advised against that plan. The South Island was just too big to see on our short two-week vacation. Short for them, really long for us workaholic Yanks. We were told we'd spend the entire time driving, with no time to properly see anything. We were encouraged to stay on the North Island because there was plenty to see and do there.

Well, there went our "soft" itinerary and hours of reading travel guides. We hadn't considered spending much time on the North Island, except to fly in and out, so we really were going to see New Zealand on the fly.

I fell in love with the North Island anyway. I saw beauty everywhere, and so varied! Around every turn, it seemed, the landscape changed—from seaside to super tall sand dunes, to crystal clear bays with wild dolphins, ancient forests, volcanoes. The people we met were delightful too, even making sure there was a water heater, tea, and cream in every place we stayed.

Maybe there was something to that black swan being in my sacred wheel angel reading! I would have happily moved there in a minute, except that our lives and family were back in the US, and New Zealand was not keen on foreigners moving there.

I'm sad to say that I drove my husband crazy on that wonderful trip. I was determined to communicate with the angels all the time, asking for guidance on every decision. Where should we go? What should we do? I consulted them each day, while my husband, the practical one, consulted the travel guides. My husband took all the angel jazz in stride, with an occasional roll of the eyes, which he mostly hid from me.

I also was determined to see a black swan and maybe come home with a feather as a souvenir. We did see a few black swans once, at a distance, but no feathers.

Before the trip, the angels had suggested that I look for a necklace that was made with both bone and jade. Maori necklaces, and their art in general, are intricate, symbolic, tribal, and beautiful, if you like that style. Which I did.

I took every opportunity to scour gift shops across the North Island, looking for a piece that fit the angels' description. Oddly, I saw none that combined those materials. There were many pieces carved from antlers and many from jade, but none that had both.

I began to question the guidance given. But just before going home, I tried one more shop. Wouldn't you know it? There it was, a pendant made from deer antler, with a small round piece of jade embedded in it. It was in a spiral shape, and in the Maori tradition, it was called a *koru* and symbolized new life. I fell in love with it and thanked the angels for encouraging me to look for this unique piece.

After we got home, I took some time off before looking for a new job. I just could not face going back into a corporate environment. I was still reeling from being downsized, unappreciated for the long hard hours I put in, and humiliated publicly in those final meetings. Just the thought of working again in a corporate environment literally nauseated me. Killing myself to generate profit for an unappreciative, faceless corporate entity no longer held any attraction for me. I absolutely could not go back.

I needed something drastically different in my life, but I didn't know what it was. I just knew that I very much wanted to apply my efforts to helping make the world a better place. Perhaps the angels could show me how. Perhaps this was my motivation to metaphorically crawl up that last twig.

Thankfully, my severance package enabled me to take some time off. With the kids embarking on new chapters in their lives, and my husband working on the other side of the country, I rattled around our big house all by myself. Empty house, empty life. I was emptying myself to make room for new experiences.

I had always been a list maker, good at filling my day with things to do, checking things off the list, done, complete, accomplished. Sitting around was for other people. But now I had time, not much on my to-do list, and no one to talk to.

Being a bit jaded with humankind at that moment, with my life completely without structure or direction, I reached out for whatever guidance I could find. I felt the angels would be a trustworthy source and hopefully willing to point me in the right direction.

About that time, a former colleague, also downsized, gave me a copy of the book *The Purpose-Driven Life* by Rick Warren. Excellent timing. It was a good time to assess and understand my purpose, sort of like creating a plan for the rest of my life, rather than just grabbing whatever job popped up.

Well, it stirred things up inside me, that's for sure. It was a very Christian book. Not that that's a bad thing. In fact, I was quite the Jesus Freak at one time too, back in middle and high school.

I was raised Presbyterian, with a mental image of God as an old man in a big chair somewhere up in the sky— sort of like the Lincoln Memorial in the air. Distant, demanding respect, unapproachable, hopefully kind. I grew up believing that I must earn my place in heaven by doing good works and living a good life.

In eighth grade, I came down with mono. I was quite sick, sleeping all day and night for weeks. During that illness, I somehow befriended Jesus, of all people. He kept me company during those long days alone in my room.

I remember how open and friendly Jesus was to me. A best friend, another invisible friend. But a very special one. In my mind's eye, I saw us walking along a beach, waves gently lapping the shore to our left. Walking and talking, like two old, best friends. It was not a long-playing mental video. Just a snippet. But it is as vivid today as it was back then. It was a deep confirmation of the nature of the very personal relationship I was beginning to have with this Son of God back then. This amazing friend.

Mono was another blessing in disguise, another call to follow a different path. My teenage life was deeply changed after that, dumping my horny, pushy boyfriend and walking to class every day with a denim-covered bible in my stack of books. A little light reading between classes.

I also got very involved in the church's youth group. Instead of just going because my parents made me, I became an enthusiastic participant, maybe even one of the unofficial leaders. I went to bible studies early in the morning before school. I had new friends, started hanging out with the older high schoolers, and a few college and post-college folks—super nice people, all of us sharing an intense love of God and Jesus.

One day, a group of us had planned to meet at the front of the church for a bible study. For whatever reason, I wasn't notified that the meeting had been called off. I hung around the church for a while, and then someone new drove up. A guy, maybe in his twenties. I thought he was there for the meeting too, so I showed him around the church and talked about our group, offering wide-open friendship to a new member.

Except he wasn't there for the meeting. He started grabbing me and kissing me, right there in the church. With no one else around, I got really scared! Somehow, as politely as my fifteen-year-old self could, I extracted myself from his unwanted attention and told him I had to go home. Fortunately, he let me go. I walked across the field in front of the church briskly, not wanting him to chase after me. When I was out of sight of the church, I ran like hell for home, which was only half a mile away. I was shaking and crying by the time I got there.

Mom and Dad were upset too when they heard what had happened, and what could have, but didn't, happen. They called the leader of the group. Several of my friends came over and apologized for not letting me know the meeting was cancelled and for putting me unintentionally in harm's way.

I settled down and was okay—on the outside. But I stopped going to the meetings. Maybe not right away, but I stopped. I dropped out of Youth Club and the "in" crowd, and they let me go. I was done with the Church, done with false friends, and done with Jesus, who in my young teenage mind I blamed for what happened that day.

Years later, after my first marriage ended and I moved back to my hometown with my two-year-old son, I thought I'd do the right thing and get us both back into the church. It's what a proper parent should do, right?

We got all dressed up. I took him to the Sunday school room, but he would have none of it. He did not want to go in. He did not want me to leave him. Separation anxiety created a very loud little boy meltdown in the middle of the hall, in the middle of the church. I knelt beside him to calm and reassure him that everything was going to be alright, that he would have fun.

He proceeded to vomit all over me. Literally, all over me. I was dripping vomit from my hair to my Sunday shoes. Without another word, I scooped him up and went home. I don't think I even tried to clean up the mess. I never went back, except for weddings or funerals. I took it as a very clear sign that "church" was definitely not for me, and apparently not for my son either.

So, that's why the *The Purpose-Driven Life* book kicked up some dust for me. I still wasn't talking to Jesus, and I was not loving the churchy talk in its pages. But I really did want to know about my Purpose, so I kept reading.

I read that my purpose comes from God. I could accept that because He created me. The Purpose fits into a larger, cosmic picture. I was okay with that too. There was a strategy and a plan. Good. The final piece (in my head, not the book) was whether I chose, or not, to cooperate and actively seek out that purpose, and then stay focused to make it happen.

I spent a *lot* of time wondering and soul-searching for my purpose. Supposedly my Higher Self, my soul, knew. But I was in the dark. Trying to trust, I would become still, eventually finding my way back to that quiet place, where I could attain some sense of peace and happiness, willing myself not to obsess on my unknown and uncertain future.

Chapter 4: The Gathering

During those post-work weeks, I searched the internet for anything on spiritual topics, even shamanism, chakras, and our energy bodies. I also stayed in touch with Connie, the angel reading lady. She told me that she would be hosting a "Gathering" within driving distance of my home and invited me to come. Because she lived in Washington State, and I was in Florida, I thought it would be a great opportunity to meet her and continue learning about angels. The Gathering would include several sessions with the angels and other fun activities.

I drove to Tampa and met a small group of very different, very nice people. None of these folks were rich, but that clearly didn't matter to them—or to me. They were definitely not stressed about deadlines, advancement, or being politically correct. Refreshing.

Life had an odd way of flowing with them. Things just happened, fell into place easily, without the detailed planning and execution that was my normal MO. We all got along well, and I even slept on the floor with them in a rather crowded hotel room.

We went to the beach early on the first morning, where Connie opened the event with a channeling. This was to be the general pattern followed each day of the Gathering: have a reading, do a little activity, have another reading, relax.

At one point, I suggested that we move the meeting from the hotel to my home, which had plenty of rooms and space, and no one was there. And I had a very nice pool. And it was free. Everyone enthusiastically agreed, and the meeting was moved.

This was not the only Gathering that Connie had held. All the other attendees were very familiar with Connie, the angels she channeled, and the format of the Gatherings. Being new and quite curious about the angels' messages and hungry to discover a new direction for my untethered life, I volunteered to transcribe the sessions and share the notes with the other attendees. The excerpts below came from those notes.

Angelic Council

We are present. We are a council of angels that works through this vessel (meaning Connie) to bring information to make your lives, basically, exactly what you would design them to be. Our help is offered to you if you are willing to receive it. You must give us permission to help you. We cannot interfere in your lives without your direct permission.

You don't have to get on your knees, fold your hands, and say a prayer that way. A simple thought is a form of prayer. The more full of love and light, the more full of openness and willingness that that thought is, the more you will manifest your heart's desire. Remember your heart's desire must not be just some vague, wish-I-had-it sort of thought. When you believe that it will improve your experience in the now, then it becomes a heart's desire, and you will have a legion of angels a thousand strong watching.

You'd be surprised what qualifies as a heart's desire. It can be the simplest thing: I want a hug from this person, or I'd love to have a moment to talk with this person, I haven't seen this person in years, it doesn't matter what. What matters is that you are willing to allow it to happen.

The Angel Michelle

Enchante. (She speaks with a French accent.) This is Michelle. It is beautiful to be with all of you this day. This is a very wonderful time for healing the body, mind, and spirit. Laughter is very important. I want to encourage you to open to the joy and love that is within you. It is your nature to be joyful beings. It is because of the modern world that you're in stress too much.

Experience life with an open heart, and in your heart trust in yourself. You tend to think too much that you can figure everything out with your intellect. All you do is twist yourself up in knots doing that. When you get stressed, try and do something to lighten yourself up. Go to a card shop and read funny cards, watch funny movies, anything that will bring a lightness into your being. Even just running and laughing will help.

You have to force and push yourself out of the heavy muck to feel the joy. So, I encourage you very much to laugh, be silly, be the little girl inside you. She knew how to play, she knew how to enjoy life, she knew how to shut out everything else and have fun in her little world.

The Angel Terran Michael

The next channeling was from Terran Michael, who is a teaching angel affiliated with Archangel Michael. I include his entire teaching below because he guided us through a past-life rewrite, in case you wish to follow along and do this for yourself.

I am Terran Michael. We are going to begin a process that we call a rewrite. You will be going into a deep meditation, picking a particular energy within the body, casting it out into the soul's garden, and then following it to discover a moment from your past that is causing you distress. Through this process, you will be able to rewrite that memory and bring healing to you.

You will go to the very first time your soul encountered that feeling. For example, if you had a betrayal that happened or an expectation from someone, and they did not complete that expectation, or they went in another direction... they hurt your feelings. We ask that you not necessarily go into this lifetime with that experience but rather go to the first time your soul had this experience, likely in a previous lifetime. In this way, it's like a domino chain. Once you heal the first hurt, you will neutralize any other similar experiences from that point on.

We will guide you step by step into the soul's garden, allow you to have your experience with a healing angel, then bring you back to the physical body. The space where the trauma resided in your body will be filled with healing energies.

Please get comfortable. You don't have to be lying down. If you choose to lie down, that's fine as well, but we do want you to be comfortable so that you are not focused on your body during this process. You can go back and repeat these steps without us anytime. You would simply walk your soul through the steps that you're about to learn to return to the garden. Each time you do this, you will have a different experience.

So, to begin the process, close your eyes and take three deep breaths. Now when we use the word visualize, we don't necessarily mean see it. We mean feel it. Visualize is a simple term for only one of your senses. You may use all of your senses as you take this journey today.

To begin with, visualize a cave opening. This cave is the entrance to your soul. Visualize walking into the cave. It's bright enough inside that you can see where you're walking. You will see a beautiful, large, wide wooden staircase. This leads down to the garden of the soul. Put your hand on the handrail or simply walk down. We will count you down, step by step, allowing you to relax more and more with each step taken, and become more focused on experiencing the energy of your own soul.

So, starting with the top step, counting down ten, stepping down nine, stepping down, you are very secure, very relaxed, knowing that you're going to the safest place that could ever exist in the universe for you. Stepping down eight, stepping down seven, allowing your body to relax, and bringing all the focus to your heart, behind the heart, that energy that you're very much into now, the energy of your soul. Stepping down six, stepping down five, stepping down four, stepping down three, stepping down two, stepping down one.

Stepping out now into the garden, you'll see an incredibly bright sunshiny day in this part of the garden. It may even feel quite hot. This is the really bright, aware, connected energy of your soul. Give yourself a moment to walk around, to see the details of your garden. No two gardens are alike because they are unique to your soul.

If you have well-manicured places in your garden, then pay attention to the flowers that are growing there. For example, a rose bush carefully tied to a trellis may represent unconditional love, but it is somewhat restricted. This is not the time to change it, just acknowledge it. Also pay attention to the scent of the rose. Is it something strong and powerful, or subtle? Is the color vibrant or subdued?

There will be areas in your garden that are wild and completely untrimmed. Pay attention if you choose to return in the future so that you can recognize your garden. Pay attention to the trees. Are they in flower or are they bearing fruit? Look at the grasses. Are they tall, rye-like grasses or wheat grasses, or are they short little clipped, hybridized grasses? Allow yourself to learn about this part of your garden. It is beautiful, spectacular. It is deeply connected to the light of heaven.

Now, you will notice to the right that there are three large stone steps. Each time you step down one of these steps, you're going to drop ten times deeper within. Ten times deeper inside the soul, that takes you to a level where you can connect to the healing angels. The garden will change as you drop down into this deeper energy.

So, as you move to the right and stand at the top of the steps, take another nice breath and allow yourself the courage to go down into these deeper areas, knowing that you will get very much in touch with information from your soul. Not something to be feared, but rather an opportunity to be viewed and rewritten as necessary.

Starting on the top step, we are going to count you down the three steps, knowing that you're going to drop ten times deeper with each step. Starting with the top, three, stepping ten times deeper within, two, stepping ten times deeper within, one, stepping ten times deeper within.

Now, you'll notice this part of the garden is very shaded. It's still very warm, but it's not hot. Very comfortable. All the flowers here are pastel shades. The smells, like honeysuckle, are sweet, but soft, and they only come on the wind. When the wind moves, you get a whiff of it and then it's gone. A very gentle part of the garden. Notice the hedges and the trees and the springs and the different places to sit and rest in this part of the garden.

Off to the left, you notice there are three more stone steps. So, as you start at the top of these steps, we're going to walk you again ten times deeper within, with each step down. Starting from that top step and counting you down, three, stepping ten times deeper within, two, stepping ten times deeper within, and one, stepping ten times deeper within.

Now as you step forward into your soul's garden, you will notice that this is a very shady part of the garden. Very relaxing. Notice that there are many stone benches, wooden benches, tree swings, rocking chairs. There are all sorts of places to sit down and rest the physical body while you do your spiritual work. Walk over to the most comfortable place for you and simply sit down. Let your body relax, it's automatically going to go into a maintenance mode.

Now a healing angel will come to you, always dressed in a pale shade of pink, indicating that you have connected to a healing angel in this space. As the healing angel walks up to where you are seated, she will simply take your physical hands and lift your spirit body straight up out of the physical form.

As the spirit body stands beside the angel, she is going to help you start scanning your body. You want to make sure that you scan completely top to bottom and then bottom back up to top. Go slowly.

What you are looking for is an area where your body wants to release some energy. It may be in the brain and all its thinking. It could be in the solar plexus where you store anger and frustration. It could be the energy of the feet and having to walk the path that others tell you.

There is no one place where the energy will be the same for each of you. So, we're asking you to each look, individually, as you scan. We're just going to keep continuing with this conversation for a few seconds, so you have time to scan the body. If you think you're into the brain, and questioning it, just step back and say, "I know." Just step back into your spirit body and say, "I know." And as soon as you allow yourself to know, you'll know where that energy pocket is.

So now the energy is identified for each of you, the angel is now going to stick her hands into your physical body. She's going to draw out the energy. With your spirit hands, help her by patting the energy until it forms a ball. It won't take a long time, but you just want to go around and keep patting it.

It may get small, it may stay large, it doesn't matter, now that the energy is free of your physical body.

The angel is going to take it from your spirit hands now and throw it into the garden. Remember that you are in your spirit body and so you can float or fly or run or skip or however you need to follow the ball. Follow that ball of energy until it leads you down into that place in the garden that relates to where that energy came from.

Now, very slowly, don't try to fight this, stay in the energy of "I allow myself to know." Just stay in it, and just know. Start first with the simple basics. Am I alone or am I with others in the place that my soul has taken me to? Is it dark or light? It could be daytime; it could be night. It could be an entirely different planet, and the colors could look very different. Don't question it, just stay in the energy. You're back to the very first time your soul has encountered this energy.

Now, allow yourself to experience this just as if you were watching a movie. What happened? What was the situation that your soul wants to rewrite? Is it a traumatic situation? Is it a sad situation? Let yourself see the details. Let the tape of this memory run forward as long as it needs to until you see the moment of the experience. Now, stop the tape, the memory, and rewind it back before that moment of trauma. Rewind it all the way back to a place where you feel comfortable. When you get to that moment, then stop.

Now, as the tape moves forward again you already know what the outcome is going to be. If you choose, you may now change and rewrite the energy of that same moment. For example, if you saw a battle, you can go back to when the parties first dis-

agreed, before they ever went to war, and rewrite the energy. If it is a personal attack, go back and trust that your intuition would have told you there was going to be trouble for you and just go back and rewrite it, trusting your own intuition to keep you out of harm's way.

Remember it must fit your moral and ethical beliefs. Do not try to rewrite anything just to quickly get it over with. Rewrite it in such a way that you feel completely comfortable.

After you feel you have completed it, ask yourself is there anything else about this situation that I need to rewrite? If there are any other steps in this process that want to be rewritten, allow them to be changed as well.

Now allow yourself to go back in the garden in front of the bench in your spirit body, with your angel beside you. She's going to pour from a beautiful pitcher into the body enough pink liquid light to fill that space to the point where it overflows with the change.

For example, if you learned to trust your intuition, she's going to fill every molecule, every subatomic structure in the body with that energy of trust. If you went back and helped someone arbitrate so that you didn't have to go to war, realize that you made a huge shift in seeing alternative ways of handling issues and that is what you brought back to the body.

No matter what the issue is, there is a beautiful pink healing light that is overflowing from the body, flooding the entire surface of your skin and permeating through everything in your body. Now breathe that pink energy throughout your body.

Remember you can repeat this process privately as many times as you like to rewrite other things in your body.

Now, we will do another scan, but this time it is simply to reclaim your soul's joy and bring it back with you into this physical life. So, do another scan of the body with your spirit eyes, from top to bottom and from bottom to top, looking for a bright light within you. For many of you, but not all of you, it will be very close to the heart. It's like a golden door. Your angels are saying this space has been identified, so simply allow your spirit body to step into that tiny little space.

Once you are in that intense and beautiful light, allow yourself to open your shoulders, rolling them back just slightly, giving your energetic wings a chance to fall open, just as if you had giant butterfly wings on your back.

Allow yourself to open to that now, to see the experience, whether you're celebrating as a conquering hero, whether you are celebrating as a spiritual being, or a spiritual teacher, whether you are celebrating some sort of accolade or you simply felt at one with nature and so good. Let your soul go back to that moment. There is no one right feeling here.

Now think of this energy as existing in every molecule in your body. As it gains momentum by picking up other moments of joy, let it spiral out from your root chakra and carry this energy not only to every molecule in your body, every subatomic structure but to everyone in the room. Share that joy with everyone in the world. Share that joy from your soul, from your energy. Everyone in the Milky Way galaxy shares that joy and that energy.

The healing angel is now going to kneel in front of your physical body and allow your spirit body to sit back down inside the physical. The healing angel is going to ask you to turn your palms upward, skyward, and as she draws little configurations or patterns or symbols on your hand, she's going to open you to a very particular energy vibration. Give yourself permission to remember these symbols. They are extremely personal symbols. Let your body resonate with the energy of the symbols you've been given.

Feel the energy as it's coming back now from the milky way galaxy to you, feel the shower of light that is penetrating the physical body, your spirit body and your mental body... all of you, still sitting there in the garden of your soul.

Now we invite you to bring the entirety of this experience of your soul, the release of the past, and the memory of joy back into your physical awareness. We will count from one to five, counting upward. With each number, you're becoming increasingly more aware of your surroundings, more awake and more alert. At five your eyes will open, you will feel refreshed, renewed and full of the joy that has been mirrored back to you from all the beings of Light, all the way back to the Galactic Center.

Beginning one, becoming more physically aware of the sensitivity of your skin and the temperature of the room, two, becoming aware of others around you, three, becoming aware of the ability to move and stretch your body, rolling your shoulders and your neck slightly, four, becoming very aware, and five, eyes open and wide awake.

Blessings to you, now and always. Know that you are love.

This meditation was extraordinary. I had never experienced anything like that, and it took a while for me to come out of the beautiful space he had led us into. Before too much time passed, though, I wrote down what happened for me in the meditation.

I got into a meditative state and calmed my mind. I entered the garden, where wildflowers—daisies, coneflowers, etc. greeted me on either side. Here it was so sunny and bright, warm, bumblebees droning amidst the flowers in happy delight.

To the right, there were three steps down, each step taking me ten times deeper within. The landing area was shady, with a bench to sit on under overhanging branches of a large maple tree. To the left there were three more steps—each again taking me deeper into my soul.

At the bottom, it opened out to a large lawn. Along the left was a very long reflecting pool with an old cement bench next to it. As I sat down, a healing angel came to me. I stepped out of my physical body into my spiritual body, which was shimmering pink. She scanned me top to bottom for signs of trauma and found a dark brown spot in the right side of my back. She reached in, gently removed it, turned around, and threw it.

I chased after it, floating, flying actually, and found it lying on the neatly manicured grounds of a castle. I looked down and saw that I was dressed as a French nobleman of perhaps the 17th century. I was in a white suit—very upper class. Someone, a colleague, came quietly up behind me and stabbed me in the back, right where that dark spot was. My feelings were of surprise and betrayal.

I was told to "rewind the tape" to uncover more of the story and then rewrite it for a better conclusion. I discovered that I was part of the king's court and closely aligned to the king, which gave me power that the other noblemen were jealous of. The king listened to my counsel, and I could turn his opinion in whatever way I chose. I never made any attempt to befriend the other noblemen. I had all I needed with the king's ear. This is why one of them killed me.

To rewrite this, I changed the dynamics of my relationship with my peers. I made sure to include them, and be included, in the everyday activities and conversations. In this way, I did not isolate myself from them or cause any reasons for jealousy.

That experience was remarkable and taught me that we can heal ourselves in unconventional ways. The use of breathing, meditation, intuition, and imagination can lift away old wounds, even ones we didn't realize we were still carrying, even from past lives. Acknowledging my misdeeds and choosing to rectify them actually mattered and could make a difference in my present or future life.

The parallel of my past life issues with my recent conflict with the sales team was not lost on me. Fortunately, this time around, it did not cause my physical death, just the death of my career, and that of my old life.

Shamanic Death

In another channeling, the Galactic Grandmothers, a group of ancient feminine souls from across the galaxy, guided us through a shamanic death experience. I had no inkling what a shamanic death was, but if it helped birth a new beginning into my life, I was all for it.

I also share this one with you in its entirety so that you can replicate the experience for yourself, if you desire. The singing/chanting mentioned was beyond my hearing, but you might want to put on some meditative Native American music to do this.

This is the time to take the sacred journey of a shamanic death. We ask each of you to go deep inside. Connect with the animal guide that comes forward to meet you.

This animal will tear away your flesh. Scatter your bones. This animal's child will come and remake you, birth you, into a new energy.

We will sing, or you might call it chanting, the power words of medicine until you are finished. Let yourself sit beside a stream or pond or lake. Allow your body to be torn apart and then rebuilt.

This visualization shook me. I did not know that I would be killed, even symbolically, and it really upset me. It took all I had to keep going and see it through to the end.

We are to do a shamanic death ritual. I don't know what that means, but everyone else seems cool with it. So, okay, here we go.

We get into a meditative state, finding stillness. We are instructed to go deeper within and find our power animal. Mine is the mountain lion who waits for me outside my cave. (The same cave as the one I entered to do the rewrite.)

"Now, allow it to kill you and tear you limb from limb."

WHAT? I was not expecting this! I am really upset and betrayed that my power animal would turn on me and do this, but it seems to be an important step. I try not to dwell on the details and visualize myself dead with my innards eaten away. Very disturbing!

A mountain lion cub comes out of the cave and creates a new me. I see light forming over my old body, and out of the spinning light, I emerge as a young child with blonde hair blowing in the wind. I have a short, ratty dress on and bare feet. I look around in wonder and puzzlement.

Now we are told to look for the Council Fire of the Galactic Grandmothers.

I see a large bonfire in what looks like a very large cave. It's off to my right a bit. Beyond the fire, I see many people sitting, the council of Grandmothers. Their faces are lit up by the flames of the fire. One at a time, we are called to the Council to be given our shamanic name. Mine is "Butterfly who Sits on a Rose." I am told that butterfly represents transformation and rose represents unconditional love.

The Grandmothers say, let go of attachments to the past. Let go, heal the loss, move on, and tell me that I stand at a crossroads, bravely facing the future. I need to know that I do not walk alone. I always have access to guidance and assistance. I just have to ask.

The shamanic death was an unsettling meditation, but it was also one that helped me feel like I crossed deeper into a new life that I never looked for, expected, or could imagine. Interestingly, I did not think about the caterpillar—chrysalis—butterfly symbolism until many years later, but as I wrote about this time in my life, I could finally see the perfection in being given such an unusual shamanic name.

Chapter 5: Getting to Know the Angels

After the gathering was over, I was even more committed to exploring what this world of angels and guides had to offer me. An unseen, but very much alive and interesting inner world was opening up to me. So many unusual experiences, but in hindsight each expanded my understanding of what was possible, helped me redefine what was real, and heal some long-held issues from the past. All was intended, I later realized, to prepare me for the future.

Always the angelic messages were supportive, but not always were they dripping with flowery, loving words. After pestering them once too often for guidance on mundane things in my life, such as looking for work, they told me,

> *Don't keep asking our opinion on every little thing. It's your life. If you want to send a resume, go ahead.*

I wanted to get to know Archangel Michael better. His presence was always unmistakable. It was like when someone with a big personality walks into a room. You just feel it. It was like that, but even more so. I guess that's why he is an *Arch*angel. His personality is intense. No frivolous conversation. His conversations are short and to the point.

Michael had a bit of an edge too. But he *is* a warrior after all. Warrior of the Light and Protector of Women and

Children. Have you seen the movie *Michael*? It is a pretty accurate portrayal. I saw a painting once of Michael riding a Harley. One bad-ass dude. It was perfect.

He really is amazing. When he was with me, I felt myself enveloped in a huge, powerful, dense, and loving presence. He was one of the very best teachers I ever had—inspiring and pushing me to do more than I ever thought possible, helping me to see things from a different perspective.

For example, one day I was once again caught up in the dramas of the day with little annoyances taking on out-of-proportion significance. I closed my eyes and sought stillness, wisdom, asking Michael to please show me the way beyond this unhelpful anxiety.

Archangel Michael, and George, showed up in my mind's eye and whisked me away to the top of a very large outdoor stadium. Think football stadium, but the biggest one you can imagine. We sat in the very top row, Michael on my left, George on my right. It felt chilly, like fall. Appropriate, I suppose, for a football game.

But it was not football. It was a play, a drama, taking place far, far below. It was so far away that I needed binoculars just to make out what they are doing.

Michael said:

> *That game "down there" is the drama, the little annoyances you were so upset about. Pull back, pull away from all of life's little dramas. They will slow you down, distract you, keep you from being open to all that your life could be. Become aware of what energizes you, and what does not. Find ways to direct your focus and attention more and more on the energizing things, and less or none on the draining things.*

That was my lesson. Right there. Distance myself from the dramas of everyday—my own invented dramas, drama inflicted upon me from others, and drama reported on the news. Find neutrality and objectivity, and from there I could find clarity and the insight to choose my response to any given situation.

Michael said it was another step toward self-mastery—to choose, to stop myself from instinctively reacting to a stimulus. Instead, taking a moment, or many, maybe days or weeks, depending on what it was to allow the whirlwind of emotions and thoughts to sift and settle. Breathe. Then, and only then, choose my response. Move from unconscious instinctive *reactions* to conscious, thoughtfully chosen *responses*. As often as I could.

I thought about the angels' advice to clarify my heart's desire. I wished I knew what it was. I felt like so much of my life was out of my hands. But the one heart's desire I was crystal clear on was to be an instrument of God. I didn't know what that meant exactly, but I wanted my life to mean something more than generating profit for a corporation. I wanted my life to make a difference in the world. Maybe my Scouting parent's motto of "Leave a place better than you found it" rang true all the way to the core of my being. Maybe I could leave the Earth, America, Florida, Orlando, or anywhere I happened to be a little better than I found it.

It was surprisingly hard for me to say what I wanted. I could not get clear on my heart's desire. Maybe I was being asked to trust that the universe had it all under control—that the universe actually knew better than I where and what I should be doing. Could I allow myself to be led blindfolded into the unknown? Could I trust that everything would work out okay? Or was I just deluding myself and making a complete fool of myself?

I didn't know what to do, or how to feel, or what actions, or non-actions, to take. I asked for clarity and guidance. Once again, Michael shared his wisdom with me:

Back away. Detach. Remember you are a spiritual being having a human experience. Relax! Pull your power and energy back into yourself, back into your truth and essence. Stop giving it away in fear and worry. Focus on your heart center.

Forgive yourself for all shortcomings. Love yourself. You are a unique expression of divinity. Know that all is perfect. Your lessons are progressing nicely. Perfect timing and divine will are in effect. All is well. Stop and feel this.

Pick a visualization—a fish jumping into the river, joining your voice to a choir, whatever works for you to know that you are aligning your life and your energy with the universe. Hold this image of unity and flow in your mind and heart. Feel the presence of your angelic support team as they surround you.

Release all your fears and worries once again. Feel the angels take your burdens from you. Today you don't have to carry them. Do this every day. You don't ever have to carry them, but you will forget and pick them up again. So do this little visualization every day to remind yourself.

In gratitude, I knew once again that things were okay and being handled. I had not been abandoned. I aligned myself to divine will, knowing that greatest good and highest joy would result, and I relaxed into the flow.

During another conversation with Michael, he offered me this advice:

Grace and kindness should be your hallmark.

Remember to remember all those who have aided and loved you, both past and present and continue to hold in gratitude those who will help and love you... even those teachers sent to you with difficult lessons to teach.

Love all things about your life—especially the challenging times and circumstances. They call forth some of your greatest growth.

That was a good reminder to mind my thoughts and attitude. I probably should have had it tattooed on me.

Taking these inner journeys and discovering the ability to heal the past, speak with nonphysical beings, and gain wisdom opened me to a much larger and very interesting world. My explorations online, through books and conversations with friends led me to explore the concept of shamanism. I learned how to meet an animal guide. There were many animals introduced to me during my sacred wheel reading, and the idea of having an animal guide was intriguing. I decided to follow the guidelines and meet *my* animal guide. Using the techniques I'd learned from other meditations, I moved into stillness and receptivity.

I visualized a cave with a triangular opening. I was immediately met by the same mountain lion from my earlier visualization. What a lovely surprise and wonderful opportunity to get to know him better.

I bumbled my way through this first meeting. I had forgotten to think of a question, so I quickly asked if he was my power animal. He said, "You know the answer to that." I apologized, thought again, and asked if my thoughts about exploring shamanism for me were on target, and he said, "You know the answer to that too."

I thanked him and asked to have a teacher or mentor come help me learn the way of the shaman. He told me I have that too (the website I had found). Oh dear. I thanked him for coming so quickly and apologized for wasting his time on questions I should have known the answers to. Rookie!

Clearly animal guides were not at all like angels. It was expected that I prepare myself with specific inquiries before seeking him out. Respect was also important. Animal guides were not play-things. They were powerful teachers and allies, and they deserved to be treated as such.

Over time, I learned the proper protocol and best ways to interact, not only with this lion, but with other animals who showed up at various times in other meditations. I found that it is possible to have more than one animal guide, or totem, and it is possible for one teacher to stop working with me, and another to take its place when I was ready to learn their lessons.

I learned about pendulums and how to use them for clearing energies and for gaining guidance. My pendulum was a good teacher and taught me how to get out of the way and allow inner wisdom to move it. Pendulums can provide simple yes/no answers to neutrally asked questions. However, I found that if I really wanted a YES, I could move it in the YES pattern with the power of directed thought.

Friends who were adept at using pendulums, or muscle testing (same thing, different technique), made it clear that it is not appropriate or effective to ask questions about yourself. If you really wanted a particular answer, you were not in neutrality and therefore could unintentionally override any information that might otherwise have been offered.

Like approaching an animal guide, the questions posed to the pendulum needed to be thought out before asking. There was little tolerance for trivial questions that I could find the answer to myself. When I began to rely too heavily on mine, even for choosing items at the grocery store, it stopped working. Dead. It had become a crutch. The message was clear.

All the answers are already inside you. Put the pendulum away.

Later on, I rarely could get a pendulum to work for me, except to occasionally show its capabilities to someone else. But it was clear that I was not to use it anymore.

Instead, I was encouraged to develop the stillness needed to recognize and hear that small inner voice. It provided better guidance and was not restricted to simple yes or no answers. Often what I heard or sensed was not at all what I expected, or what I wanted to hear. Often, I did not really like the answer. As with all things, it was up to me to decide to listen to it, or not. Follow the suggestions, or not.

Chapter 6: Looking for Answers in Unlikely Places

I was honored when Connie invited me to come to her home in Seattle for some intense healing work with her friend Hazel—sort of a one-on-one Gathering with healing work included. She felt it would help move me past the trauma of losing my job and step forward into a new chapter of my life. Sounded pretty good to me.

In preparation for the trip, however, Connie said that the angels recommended that I visit a battleground before coming out. There apparently was a past life that needed to be healed. Their advice was often maddeningly vague, but I was learning that it was up to me to figure out what they meant.

Honestly, before the Florida Gathering, I had never thought about having a past life. I wasn't sure there was such a thing. It definitely was a significant departure from the Presbyterian teachings I grew up with, where life was a one-shot deal, followed by an express train to the big mansion with many rooms somewhere up there—if you were lucky and passed Judgment. Otherwise ...

And although I was hungry and curious for a different life, this assignment was a stretch. My whole career was founded on objective analysis and concrete data, so a topic as out there as a past life that needed healing certainly triggered some skepticism. Yet, the past life rewrite we did at the Gathering was real enough and illuminating. Hopefully healing.

Because I wasn't sure what my life should look like or what I should be doing, I had to find the courage to look for answers and discover new directions for my life in unlikely places. Much like that very first angel reading, I went along with the guidance, taking this new battleground assignment as seriously as I could, with a "wait and see" attitude.

Past life? Healing? I had so many questions, like how would I know who I was in that past life? What needed to be healed? How would I go about healing it? How would I figure it all out? Which battlefield? Which war? Couldn't I just do a past life rewrite like we did at the Gathering? Why did I need to go there?

Now, I *hate* war and anything that closely resembles it. Making plans to visit a battleground would *never* be on my list of things to do. It was definitely an unlikely place to find answers. But hey, stay open and curious, Kath.

I did some research, starting with the basics. What is a "past life"? My experience with the rewrite was interesting, but I wanted to know more. I learned that many religions and philosophies believe in past lives, the premise being that consciousness never dies, and some invisible, eternal, aspect of us has lived at least one, maybe more, lifetimes in the past and will continue to do so after the present life is over.

I also learned that traumas or situations that happened to us, or more importantly that were caused by us, in previous lives carry forward to impact our present or future lives. I dealt with the seventeenth-century nobleman-me and saw the parallels to this life. I guess I would see what the unknown soldier-me needed to address. Anything to get my life onto a new forward trajectory.

I discussed my proposed adventure to a battlefield with a friend who was a history buff. He was intrigued, and with the few clues given to me by the angels, he gladly helped me research America's wars, battles, and key figures. (We assumed the battle took place in America because I was to go there before flying to Seattle.)

Eventually, through a lengthy process of elimination, we determined that it was the Civil War, the Battle at Gettysburg, and a past life as Lt. General James Longstreet. That was a surprise because he was a commander of the Confederate (Southern) Army, and I was a "Northerner" from New Jersey in this life.

Just to be sure, I asked the angels if our analysis was correct, and they confirmed that it was. I dug deeper to understand the life of General Longstreet, this former "me" to discover what had happened that needed healing.

He had been a well-regarded commander in the Confederate Army, at least at first. In the early battles of the Civil War, his leadership and strategies won many battles for the South. Because of his success, he was promoted to Lt. General and became one of General Robert E. Lee's most trusted field commanders.

The problem came during the Battle of Gettysburg. General Lee conferred with Longstreet about the best way to take on the Union Army there. Lee wanted to launch a direct attack. Longstreet, however, felt that it was a risky strategy due to the weakened state of the Confederate Army and the strength of the opposing army's forces. He recommended that the Confederates back away and establish a defensible position, forcing the enemy to attack them. This was the tried-and-true strategy that had won him so many battles previously.

Although the details of their conversation were never documented, it is believed that General Lee considered the logistics of relocating the entire army to be too difficult and complicated. The soldiers were already exhausted, and some key troops (including Longstreet's) had not even arrived yet at Gettysburg. In addition, the small farm roads in the area hindered a quick relocation. Clean water was limited, having already been polluted by the large military encampments. In the end, General Lee decided to stay with his original strategy and launched an offensive against the Union Army.

On the second day of battle, Longstreet's men finally arrived, and after a brief rest, joined the battle. Critics later said that this delay gave the Union General extra time to prepare for his attack. On the third day, General Lee launched his offensive, which is known today as "Pickett's Charge," an attack of over 12,500 Confederate soldiers against the Union troops.

Unfortunately, Longstreet's reservations about taking an offensive position turned out to be correct. The open field where the battle was waged offered little cover, and the Union Army shot the Confederate soldiers like fish in a barrel. Although a small number of the Confederate soldiers managed to reach the Union lines and engage in hand-to-hand combat, most were killed on the field. The Battle of Gettysburg became the turning point of the Civil War, with more than 50,000 casualties. It was the bloodiest single battle of the war.

Despite being one of the most successful Confederate generals in the Civil War, Longstreet became the scapegoat for the South, being blamed for the Confederates ultimately losing the Civil War. He is still reviled by the South to this day.

The site of the Battle of Gettysburg is now a national military park, with more than 1,000 monuments, memorials, markers, and plaques to commemorate and memorialize the men who fought and died there, even Longstreet. That was where I needed to go.

Despite all my research about Longstreet, I had no particular feelings about him one way or the other. His story did not resonate with me, and I wondered why I needed to heal this supposed past life of mine. But I was willing to find out.

In preparation for my trip, I identified where Longstreet fought key battles and made a travel itinerary. I visited the site of the Battle of the Wilderness in Virginia, which happened the year after the Battle of Gettysburg, where Longstreet was accidentally shot in the neck by one of his own soldiers. I stood on the spot where he was shot, imagining how it all went down.

I imagined all those soldiers, the weariness they carried, the horror of killing sapping their courage. I imagined the soldier loading his gun, preparing to fire at what he thought was the enemy approaching, but who turned out to be his commander, Longstreet, returning. I saw the gun firing and the bullet hitting Longstreet in the neck, the shock and chaos that followed that moment, the urgency to stop the bleeding and get him to the medics. Fortunately, he survived, but he was out of commission for a long time.

Site of the Battle of the Wilderness

The next day, I drove to Gettysburg and walked the length and breadth of the battlefield—miles and miles of walking in the brisk wintry February cold. Sitting on a rise when I first arrived, overlooking the field, time slipped away, and my mind's eye saw so many dead bodies lying on the field. I felt deeply the horror of that terrible battle, the sadness still held in the land, and now in my heart.

Gettysburg

I invited the spirit of General Longstreet, my former self, to walk with me. Together, I told him, we would find his statue. Together we would heal whatever needed to be healed, for him, and apparently for me. I found a stone about the size of a fist, and I carried it with me, all thirteen miles, to symbolize our bond and shared quest.

After several hours, I felt Longstreet becoming impatient and agitated, pressing me to find his statue. Gettysburg is a very large place, and there are statues everywhere commemorating the fallen.

Finally, I found it—tucked off to the side in a little grove, at ground level, facing away from the walking path—all symbolically implying a statue in disgrace. I almost missed it. Because he had been a Lt. General, I expected to find his statue in a more prestigious location and raised on a pedestal.

A familiar wave of emotion swept over me. Unappreciated, unfair! Ah, I finally understood. Yes, the general's emotions reflected my feelings and my life! I too was misunderstood and unappreciated for all I did in my last job. My downsizing was unfair too.

There it was, the piece that needed healing, for both of us.

We sat together, he and I, for the better part of an hour, chewing on life, and on life's little deaths, disappointments. Feeling pretty black—and blue.

Then I noticed something I'd missed earlier. Someone had left a handful of daffodils on the statue. An offering, a gesture of honor and respect. It was a simple gesture, but it was monumental, and so very welcomed, in that moment, to two smarting souls.

*Lt. General James Longstreet's Statue at Gettysburg,
with daffodils*

With the healing work on the battlefield completed, I flew on to Seattle—unsure what I would be doing
but trusting that everything would work out just right. I
looked forward to meeting Connie's friend Hazel and experiencing her unique healing work.

When I arrived in Seattle, Connie picked me up and
said we were going on a little adventure before seeing
Hazel. We went to the San Juan Islands, taking a ferry
across to Orcas Island and spending the night at a bed and
breakfast there. It was beautiful, but I was unclear why
we went, except for some sightseeing. The next day, we
headed back to the mainland.

On the ferry ride back, Connie received an impromptu angelic message that I needed to have a drum—a Native American drum. Really? I didn't even know how to drum. I had never had any interest in drumming and certainly had no need for a drum. But I was game. Seeking answers in unexpected places, right? But where could we find a drum, out here in the middle of Puget Sound?

I picked up a local advertising magazine on display in the seating area. You know the kind, listing local restaurants and places to visit and shop in the area. As I flipped through it, I found a small advertisement, all the way in the back, for a Native American shop, coincidentally in the town where the ferry was scheduled to dock shortly, around 5 pm.

On a whim, I called the shop and asked if they had any drums. The woman said yes, they had a few. I asked how late the shop was open, and she said 5. I explained our situation (being on a ferry and arriving at 5). She said that she would wait for us. Wow. How nice!

The ferry ran late, and we didn't get to the shop until after 6. My heart sank, but amazingly she had stayed for us, an hour past closing time. She welcomed us in and presented several drums for my consideration. I looked to Connie for some direction.

On the table were two drums. One had an eagle painted on the face, and the other had a bear. I took the stick and started hitting them. That's what you did with a drum, right? Hit it with a stick. Connie was horrified. NO! Hold it like *this,* in one hand, and beat it with the other, like this, with the BEATER. See? Oh.

The drums were nice and well made, but neither resonated with me. I glanced around the showroom and spotted another drum hanging on the wall. I took it down and struck it with the beater. Ah! Now THIS was a drum! It had a wonderful, authoritative "voice." Deep and strong, made with elk hide, the drum was much larger than the others. Perhaps that's why it had a big voice, and why I eventually named it "Speaker." The image on the drum was quite unusual too—reminiscent of Alaskan art, and yet not. We could not figure out what it was supposed to represent, but it didn't matter. I had already fallen in love with it. I purchased it, and we headed for Connie's home.

The next morning, when we looked at the drum again, we realized that there were in fact many images, all in what seemed to be Alaskan type symbology. Raven, owl, crane, dolphin. Dolphin? Yes. And other images too, like whale, stars, a womb, and an umbilical cord. It was a very unusual drum, to be sure!

Speaker

We finally figured out that the largest image, taking center stage, represented a black swan because of the distinctive band across the beak. It made no sense. Why would a Native American drum have an image of a New Zealand black swan on it? The animal was not native to the Americas. But mine did.

It slowly sank in that somehow this drum was made for *me*. By someone I probably would never meet. Who knows why? Perhaps one day I'd understand it. With certainty, I knew this drum was something very very special and that the angels knew exactly what they were doing when they encouraged me to find a drum while we were out there in the middle of Puget Sound.

I thought back on how it came to be in my possession. A chance suggestion. A nearby store. A lady willing to wait an hour. A glance around the room. Life was starting to get *very interesting* indeed!

Speaker was a big drum, twenty inches in diameter. How was I going to get it safely home on the plane? I needed to wrap it in something protective. Wouldn't it be appropriate to wrap it in an elk hide, since the drum's skin was made of elk hide?

Now where would I find an elk hide? It would have been unheard of in Florida, but this was Washington State, and wouldn't you know? There happened to be a tanner in Connie's town who just happened to have an elk hide for sale. Unfortunately, it was promised to another customer who was planning to pick it up the next day. Boldly I asked if it would be possible to stop by right now and pay cash for it? Surprisingly, he agreed.

The hide was soft and just exactly the right size to cover Speaker for safe passage. I had just enough cash to pay for it. Another lesson: When something was meant to be, the pieces fell into place effortlessly—and with a bit of adventurous fun. Life was *definitely* getting more interesting by the minute.

Connie put on a CD with Native American drumming music to listen to while we drove to Wenachie to finally visit Hazel. With Speaker on my lap, I learned about, and practiced, the types of rhythms and sounds the drum could make.

On the way, Connie told me that Hazel was a sound healer who could help me heal my recent traumas. I was curious what a sound healer was and how she would do whatever it was she was going to do.

We met her for breakfast the next morning. Hazel was a thousand years old, a little wisp of a woman with kind, wise eyes that saw all the way into my soul. I liked her right away. At one point, she reached across the table, over the maple syrup and pancakes, touched my heart, and asked, "Why does your heart feel like mush?" Hoo boy. Out of nowhere, a flood of tears welled up. I told her I had no idea. She smiled gently and said, "We have work to do!" I guess we did.

We met later that day in a small massage room. Turned out she was also a massage therapist, and a darn good one at that! As she massaged me with her strong yet gentle hands, she emitted the most incredible range of noises. It sounded like she was speaking dolphin or ... I don't know what! She made sounds that normally do not come out of a human mouth, and she did it with gusto! I wasn't sure what was being accomplished, but I definitely felt better when she was through.

We repeated these sessions two more times during my stay. She also recommended a few books to read, including the *Secret of the Beloved Disciple* by James Twyman (really any book by this author, she said) and *Christ Power and the Earth Goddess* by Marko Pogacnik. They were interesting titles that I promised to follow up on later.

I came to love Hazel dearly and respect her gift of healing. Just being near her made me feel better, made me want to be more like her. I was starting to realize that there would be a lot in life that I would not understand, like how she did what she did, but that wouldn't stop me from appreciating and accepting a gift and acknowledging the *love* behind the gift.

I was not quite sure what her healing sessions specifically did for me, but I do know that her kindness, skill, and commitment to the healing process made a huge impression on me. She was unapologetically herself and simply radiated love and peace and joy.

One afternoon, we picked up Connie's three grandchildren, who lived nearby, and took them to a park to play. We had a great but oh-too-short-time together.

When it was time for me to head home, Connie was instructed by Archangel Michael to perform a ceremony to anoint me as one of his warriors. She explained that I had, apparently, made a contract with Michael before entering this lifetime. She said that the details of the contract would unfold over time, and that he would be with me, guiding me along my path. After my recent experiences on the battlefield, both literally and figuratively at my job, I wasn't so sure I wanted to become a warrior.

Connie explained that being a warrior for Michael meant being a warrior of the Light. The battle I would fight would mostly be one that I waged within me—between old life, old values and new life, new values. Heartled life, or ego-led life. Light, or dark. To be Michael's warrior meant choosing the Light, as often as possible, and to shine the Light for others, as often as possible.

It would not be easy. I would have to move against the current of everyday life, of all that I had known. It would require much of me. I would need courage to face my fears. I would need to develop compassion for myself and come to accept, love, and honor myself. I would need to find the strength to walk away from that which no longer served me. I would need to develop the persistence to pick myself up when I stumble and carry on.

Awesome. So much for an easy life ahead.

Connie also explained that Michael has armor which can be used to protect women and children and that I now had permission to use it if needed. The armor consists of:

A breastplate with a hole in the heart area, which allows love to flow out but no harm to come in.

A helmet, which can be worn to protect me from other's thoughts.

A sword, which can only be used once in a particular situation. One decisive strike, from bottom to top, to cut the cords of injustice.

Then Connie asked me to become still. After a little while, she asked me to notice a unique sensation somewhere on my body. That was weird because I was feeling a distinct pressure on both temples, like someone was pushing their fingers into either side of my head, sort of like how George had once pushed on the middle of my forehead. This, it turned out, was to become Michael's way of letting me know that he was with me, whether I was in a quiet meditation, or anytime throughout the day or night.

Finally, Connie applied a dab of an essential oil on my temples, and then in the center of my forehead. And it was done. I was one of Michael's warriors.

Chapter 7: Learning How Spirit Works

After I got home from Seattle, the angels nudged me to go on a shopping adventure with them. It was an interesting experience, to say the least.

Get in the car. Head over to Longwood ... Pull into this shopping center.

WHAT? I never shop here.

Just do it.

Hmpf.

Go into that store.

The weird comic bookstore?

Yes, that one.

I had no idea why I was there, or what I was after. I calmed myself down and just rolled with it, hoping that I really hadn't gone crazy this time. I wandered around the store for a while. I saw piles and piles of comic books, comic action hero toys, posters, costumes, and other collectibles—piles of stuff everywhere.

I eventually worked my way around to a little side room and found some classic PEZ candy dispensers.

Yes, that's it!

That's it? We came here for PEZ?

Yup. Get three of them.

I picked out three, with their help, of course. It had to be just the right three. For what purpose? I had no idea, yet. I paid for them and headed home.

Stop at the grocery store. Go down the candy aisle. Pick up three sleeves of PEZ candy refills.

I didn't even know they still sold PEZ candy refills. What a weird day this was turning out to be! I headed home and packed them in one of those bubble wrap mailing envelopes, as instructed.

Send them to Connie for her grandkids.

I addressed the envelope and sealed it shut.

Run it to the post office. Now please.

(See how politely bossy the angels can be?) But I complied.

Now, here's the amazing part. The VERY NEXT DAY I got a call from Connie, thanking me for sending the little candy treats. The grandkids just loved them! I had mailed them from Florida. How that package got clear across the country, diagonally no less, *overnight*, is beyond me. But I swear it happened, just like that.

To this day I have no idea why it was important for those kids to have the PEZ. But it made them happy, and I had an interesting, odd, adventure. *And* I learned that when I get a nudge, it's best to just roll with it, logic be damned. Nothing but good would come from it.

———

At home, the days stretched out, long and quiet. Alone, with time on my hands, I relished the stillness, venturing within, seeking audience with the angels. There were moments, though, when the real world fears and anxieties bubbled up and threatened to unhinge me. I knew I "should" be looking for work, but just the thought of it turned my stomach and made me break out in a cold sweat.

Michael gave me a very clear and concise message.

You will want to rush the process. You can't. Know that this river cannot be pushed. You must surrender to its flow and timing over and over again.

Be grateful, for premature departure would be as tragic as a butterfly cut from the chrysalis too soon. Trust the process; trust the timing.

You cannot push the river.

In my mind's eye, I saw a fairly large lazy river (maybe like the Mississippi, but I've never seen it), with a lashed-together wooden raft floating on it Huck Finn style. On the raft were lounge chairs with Archangel Michael lying on one, sipping a cool drink. He invited me to join him and enjoy the scenery as the raft flowed with the river's current.

Nope! I've got this! I doggedly dog paddled next to it, trying to get "there" by my own efforts. He called out, reminding me that I couldn't push the river, couldn't make things happen any faster or take shortcuts to shorten the journey, that I would reach the far shore, the destination, at the appointed place, and at the right time.

He also told me that I would be "taken down to nothing" before the journey is over. Like hell. This I could not accept and struggled valiantly to bypass that declaration. And I tried to beat the timeline, just like I had at work. Michael laughed and told me that struggle was allowed, but not necessary.

Michael and I met, back here at the raft, with me still dog paddling alongside, many, many times over the years to come, revisiting the same lesson, over and over. It was a hard lesson for me—to release striving, to release my death grip on old beliefs. Ingrained in me from childhood, an artifact from my Protestant upbringing, was that only by working hard would I get to heaven. The idea of getting on that raft, hanging out with Michael on a comfy lounge chair and going with the flow was, literally, inconceivable for me.

For me, surrender had always been a dirty word, a word for the weak and lost, a word for the hopeless and victims of this life. And that was definitely not me.

I chewed on that word, *surrender*, for a long time. Eventually, I realized that it was not about giving up in defeat, crushed and broken. It was exactly the opposite. I penned this in my journal one morning:

> *Surrender does not mean to give up.*
> *It means to give way.*
> *To choose to step aside and allow Spirit to move as it will.*
> *Surrender requires that I learn to listen to, and trust, the Guidance given.*
> *To choose to give way to Guidance and suspend personal agenda.*
> *To respond enthusiastically and nimbly to Guidance given, without analysis, argument, or deliberation. Just immediate, unquestioned action.*
> *To go with the flow. Find and feel into the direction of the Flow, which is the Will of the Universe. Align and add my personal energy and gifts to it.*
> *Paddle with the river's current.*
> *Give way, allow Spirit to flow.*
> *Become part of the flow, let it gently move me forward.*
> *Be delivered to the next thing, rather than grasping for my desires and ambitions.*

Still, surrender was one of the hardest concepts for me to accept. It took years, and many opportunities to practice, until I could see and embrace the wisdom in it.

From the very beginning, starting with the first reading of my Sacred Wheel, and again during the Gathering, the angels encouraged me to set specific intentions for my life. They said,

> *That which you believe, you will receive. Humans need to be specific about what they want. You are responsible for your future. Please note that does not necessarily include being aligned to the will of God. That's the beauty of it. It's a choice—free will—that you must make every day.*

Okay. So, Michael advised that I go with the Divine flow. But I was also supposed to set specific intentions. To me, it was a confusing and contradictory set of instructions. Was I supposed to create a life strategy, a very detailed blueprint of how I wanted my life to be, and then wait for it to show up? Or was I supposed to float through my life on the raft one day at a time?

With no clear direction, and confusing angelic guidance, I did my best to set very specific intentions for moving my life forward in a good, aligned, spiritual way. I filled many, many journal pages with detailed intentions for starting several spiritually oriented businesses as a way to support myself while still following a spiritual path. I also outlined other details for my ideal life, like where I would live, what I would be doing, what types of people I would surround myself with, etc.

But honestly? Nothing worked. Not one clearly defined intention manifested for me. Not one. Yet I had friends who could manifest easily. New cars, work projects, etc. What was wrong with me? Either I was a spiritual idiot, or perhaps there was something I missed.

I began to realize that all the intention-setting felt very much like sending a long, detailed Christmas list to some kind of Santa Claus God. I want this, and this, and this, and I want it all right now! Did I remember to say please? (No.) And I stomped my feet impatiently. Oh dear.

In my mind's eye, I pictured the Almighty Creator, listening to my Santa Claus list of requests and intentions, listening to EVERYONE'S Santa Claus lists, 24/7/365, His weary head propped up by His fist, eyes closed. Truly, is this the best His children could do? That I could do?

And what about people setting intentions that were at cross purposes to each other? Like two people both wanting the same job, for example. How could God respond favorably to both people? Maybe that was why sometimes I got no answer, or not what I asked for? Or maybe, maybe, God knew something I didn't know, knew the bigger picture, had a better plan.

What if setting intentions and wishing for specific outcomes for my life would actually limit my life? Compared to God, I was just like an ant on a blade of grass, unable to see the yard, the sidewalk, or the world just a few inches away. On the other hand, He could see the whole landscape and knew exactly how I was meant to live within it.

What if I was missing the boat, missing the point, missing the gift? My intention setting was always about me, my life, and how *I'd* like it to be. What if, what if, from time to time, I looked at things through God's eyes? What if, instead of launching into another long list of requests, I stopped and instead asked what advice or information I needed in that moment, for that situation. Or, better yet, was there something I could do for Him? Then once asked, could I sit quietly and wait respectfully to hear the reply?

As I mulled all this over, a message from Archangel Michael confirmed my suspicions.

Follow the weave of grace in your life to this point. See how you have been loved, guided, and protected every moment. See then what is being asked of you now—to move from being a child that needs to be protected to becoming a warrior of the Light, to stand side by side, with us, *in your full power and glory to help shift the balance and manifest Heaven on Earth once again.*

You must grow up spiritually first. You wouldn't give a child a sword, would you? The child could hurt himself or others because he would not understand or appreciate its power. So it is with you. Your gift, your path, has not fully manifested yet because you are not ready to receive it. Therefore, you cannot know your work with us. We are preparing you. Timing is perfect. You haven't screwed up. All is perfectly on schedule.

Now we are asking you to face your fears. They keep you too "young," shall we say. We are also honing your ability to follow "orders" even when they run counter to logic or your nature. Being quiet and patient are not your strong suits, yet you are choosing these behaviors because we've asked you to.

You are gathering power and wisdom in ways you can't understand at this time, preparing for your work in your sleep and in your waking. We honor and appreciate your efforts—more than you know!

Imagine becoming the perfect arrow, preparing yourself for flight. You move in the opposite direction of the desired target in order to build the power needed for flight. Allowing yourself to be pulled back, nocked in the cord, and aimed by the Divine. Only Spirit knows when the arrow will fly. It's up to you to simply be ready.

At the perfect time, you will fly true, straight, and strong, hitting the bullseye perfectly. For now, do as we ask. Face your fears, follow your guidance, think as a warrior, not as a child, and practice patience for a little while longer.

I had the choice, complete free will, to continue to try and architect my life through intentions or to align with that bigger picture, to Divine Will, or not. My choice. Get on the raft or continue to dog-paddle. I crawled up on the raft.

Letting go of my need for conditions, for wanting what I wanted, was not easy. Simple, but hard. Just let go of the need to control my life. I found out just how much of a control freak I was when I started to do this, and it kept resurfacing every time I thought I had it licked. It was a process, for sure, but I had to start somewhere. No surprise, there were many times to come when I found myself in the river again, but always the invitation was there to climb aboard.

I also came to realize that God didn't owe me an explanation for anything. So often I would pray and beg to know what came next, like it was my right to know.

It took a while, but I finally caught on that I would only get the next piece of the puzzle, the next step on the path, just exactly when I needed it—and not a minute sooner. That's just the way Spirit works.

Chapter 8: Learning to Travel the Soul's Path

I had already learned that trying to forge my own path was wasted effort. But it took many years to begin to loosen my stranglehold. Feeling like I was in control of my life was comforting and reinforced by the outer world. Intentionally choosing *not* to be in control looked, and felt, like lunacy. Yet, that was exactly what was being asked, expected, and required. Walk the trail less traveled. Follow Spirit, even when it felt like life was a big game of Blind Man's Bluff.

It also taught me patience. I came to accept that God works in His own timing, which was much slower than *I* ever felt was necessary, of course. He always knows what is needed to make something happen, and He lovingly synchronizes events and timelines to manifest it effortlessly. My impatience was not His problem. It was mine.

Trust was the final lesson—to know, absolutely, that whatever was needed would come, fall into place, and be perfect. Sometimes I found that I had what was needed all along, like Dorothy's ruby shoes.

I felt strongly that my life was a gift from God. It was my fervent heart's desire to do something, or make something beautiful, with my life as my gift back to God. That became my heart's desire.

It occurred to me that I was being invited to engage with God, and all those of the Divine realm, in a deeper, more personal way. I felt I was being invited to set aside prayer, which more and more felt like a one-way conversation by me talking *at* Santa Claus God and instead to have more of a *conversation.*

I thought about what having a conversation actually meant: people taking turns speaking and listening. We all have been in a conversation when the other person goes on and on about the endless details and dramas of their life, and we can't get a word in edgewise. When I approached Santa Claus God with my requests and whining, I realized that *I* was being that annoying person. Oh dear!

I also thought about how easy it was to be sloppy in a normal conversation, just spewing out the first thing that comes to mind, digressing, losing my train of thought, maybe not really paying attention to what the other person was saying. Yet, in the presence of a teacher or mentor, I tended to choose my words a bit more carefully and listen more intently. That extra effort came from the respect I had for that person. Why wouldn't I do the same when speaking with God? There couldn't be a better mentor!

To avoid sloppy-talk with God, I realized that I needed first to have a conversation with myself to organize and clarify my thoughts before reaching out for a chat, taking time to consider and clarify what I really wanted to discuss. Only then would I put the question or concern on the table, metaphorically, and listen for a reply.

It was rare for an answer to come right away. I wasn't the Boss of God, and He didn't owe me an explanation or answer. He wasn't obliged to respond, instantaneously, or at all. But in fact, eventually, I always got an answer—sometimes in a solid gut feeling of yes or no or in a myriad of other ways, such as a song's lyrics, phone call, or even a TV show story.

And sometimes, silence. I learned that silence in itself was also an answer. Silence could mean no or not yet or something else is better, or the question did not need an answer because I already knew it but was hoping for something different.

Eventually, I understood that no words were even necessary. God was already fully aware of my thoughts, dreams, and concerns for others. I didn't have to ask for His help on anything, for myself or on behalf of another person. I could simply open myself to His Love and align myself to it. Then I could expand that Love from my heart, like a bubble, to encompass my family and friends, expand again to surround the city, the country, the planet, and finally the universe. Everything became embraced, blessed, infused, by that Love.

During that time, I read many books, seeking knowledge, information, and guidance. I was looking for a point of view to help me make sense of life and provide a lattice to grow upon. One concept I came across resonated with me. It explained how each of us makes a plan, an agenda, before we are born on this planet—sort of like a course curriculum, where the lessons we want to learn and the experiences we want to have were all set up to enhance our development as conscious beings.

The concept went on to say that living in a physical body and dwelling upon the Earth are extraordinary gifts. Not all souls are given this opportunity. It is an honor to be here. A lifetime on Earth provides a unique environment for souls to learn and grow through physicality, duality, connection, and experience. As souls, we do this over and over. One lifetime we are a king, the next a pirate, a beggar, Mother Teresa. Maybe even a toad or a pebble.

Once we are born, we get caught up with our experiences and forget about our soul and our agenda. The soul becomes a backroom concept, not our lifeline. We are like naughty kids who have attention deficit disorder, off running around and getting in trouble, living the drama and thinking that this is all there is.

One day, I realized that my soul must be incredibly patient, and probably completely exasperated, with me. It must be sighing yet again as I got distracted with the next shiny thing, or bogged down in grief, depression, and anger, forgetting who I was, or why I was here.

Feeling depressed, I went into meditation, visualizing a stone at the bottom of a stream. I was told to reach up to the highest vibrations I could access at that moment and envision the stone becoming a cork and rising to the surface.

As I did that, I simultaneously felt my energy lift into joy. Amazing. I was encouraged to stretch further still until I could access and merge with the heart and mind of God, then stretch down and do the same with the Earth, then stretch outward to the edges of the universe.

I was told I've been thinking too linearly and three dimensionally about my life, that I needed to learn to use the deep magic to make the changes desired in my life. The deep magic is Life itself, experiencing and creating itself anew. My energy lightened even more, causing me to feel almost giddy.

I decided right then to invite my soul to have its way in this life I am living now. My soul had let me have *my* way over and over, lifetime after lifetime. I figured it was time to give something back. I wanted my soul finally to have the experiences *it* wanted to have. And if I got too far off course, my soul had my explicit permission to kick my butt back in line.

As in so many of my pivotal, innocent decisions, I had no idea what I had just committed myself to. Everything was about to change, but I didn't know it at the time.

Everything that no longer served me would fall away, and new experiences would come to expand my understanding of how to work with, communicate with, and fuse with God. And along the way, I would strengthen a litany of more positive attributes, including trust, forgiveness, patience, compassion, and acceptance.

My soul kept its own counsel on the long-range view of my life, for my own good. It gave me just what I needed at the moment to keep me out of trouble, from trying to take back control, from thinking I knew what's best. It kept me curious and attentive, and flexible and responsive. And annoyed and frustrated at times.

But those became the new rules of the road as I learned to travel my soul's path. Each time I tried to go back and live by the old rules, life became full of struggle. When I kept to the new rules, my soul and I were great traveling companions, going further than I ever could have imagined and experiencing things I never would have dreamed. When I kept to the new rules, I dwelt in that "Peace that goes beyond understanding." It really exists, and it is solid, powerful, huge. It's like being a beautiful tree whose roots go deep, deep into the Light, anchored, connected, and nourished.

Inviting my soul to have its day changed my life.

Chapter 9: Creating Beauty

Lack of job, income, and direction weighed heavily on me. The war between old-world values and this new way of being was as intense and brutal as that of the caterpillar and the imaginal cells. I was at once loving the freedom and flow of my post-corporate life yet drowning in guilt that I wasn't doing my part to support my family.

I had always been an equal contributor financially and my severance had long run out. Living on half the income was beginning to take its toll on us. Although our older son was on his own now, and our younger son was overseas with the Marines, he would still need to finish college when he came home. The emotional stew inside me was toxic, and I had no idea how to resolve it.

I wanted absolutely unbiased guidance, so I scheduled a reading with Connie to ask the angels what I should be doing, hoping they could give me some clear direction.

They said I would be very busy "creating beauty." Connie said she didn't know if it was decorating or something else, but it would be beauty on a grand scale—maybe like working for a city arts council to acquire sculptures.

I didn't feel drawn to the arts council thing. I had never felt drawn to art of any kind. Still, creating beauty on a grand scale sounded interesting. It could be anything, I supposed. Creating is good. Beauty is good. The "grand scale" echoed back to the things my mother had told me when I was about three or four years old. She had my palm read (Why? I have no idea. Not something my mother was inclined to do.) But the medium told mom that I would do "great things." And according to my fifth grade teacher, I was a 'special' child. Those were all great expectations, I suppose, but without a drop of specific information. This expectation to do great things had driven me my whole life. Not knowing "what" those things were made me try to excel at everything. Now the angels were adding their two cents too. No pressure.

But as I had already started to figure out, the angels' messages were clear as mud, vague, and without tangible details I could act on. After thinking about it for a week or so, I still couldn't make heads or tails of it, so I asked for more clarification. That time the angels said that it could be sculptures—either for parks or museums. Or maybe I would be hired by a large institution to acquire and install large artwork. They affirmed that I would be well paid.

Or, they said, perhaps I might actually create the sculptures themselves—simple but inspiring pieces to help pull humanity toward peace and love—and that there would be something "Atlantean" about them. They suggested I play with that energy. Oddly, that felt much better to me. The idea of acquiring and installing art did not appeal to me at all.

Still, it was very strange advice because I had no previous interest, nor training, in art, nor had I ever had any interest in Atlantis. (Do you see a theme here? It was the same thing with the drum and drumming.) But if the angels thought it was a good idea, well, I guess it was worth checking out. I *was* seeking answers in unusual places after all.

The comment about sculptures being Atlantean definitely piqued my curiosity. What would make a sculpture Atlantean? Because I had no other path opening for me, and because I asked for, and was given, more specific information, I kept going.

I read articles online and got the general gist of the legend of Atlantis, along with the many theories about where it had existed and why it became lost. The more I read, the more skeptical I became. Some of the so-called experts were righteously adamant about their theories about the Lost Continent, and their theories were not the same!

I decided to try and figure out for myself why Atlantis was so intriguing to people. It was supposedly a golden age when people lived in peace, harmony, and enlightenment. Perhaps we secretly hoped that what was once possible could happen again, that we *could* live in peace again. Wouldn't that be delightful?

I asked my mountain lion animal guide if he had any information for me about Atlantis and this possible new direction for me. He led me deep underwater. It was so strange because it was dark blue all around me and got darker as we descended. I did not expect this at all, but then again it made perfect sense if indeed the lost continent was engulfed in the flood. I felt sadness about the time when things fell. I saw white and light-colored buildings rise up very high and ethereal. I saw a structure of two stone kings guarding the pass, like in the *Lord of the Rings*. They were tall, regal, inspiring, and a bit more stylized in my vision than in the movie.

I also got the image of Rivendell and the elves from the same movie. Didn't they have the same qualities that we attribute to the Atlanteans? They were regal, majestic, peaceful, enlightened, in harmony with the earth. Perhaps they *were* the Atlanteans, and their age ended with the flood, similar to their passing from Middle Earth. It was fanciful thinking, but who knows. There might be something to it...

I didn't find any information about Atlantean *art* in my research though, so I waited for some inspiration to get me going. I found a fascinating 3D-looking image on the internet, printed it out, and really studied it. It was composed of different sized blocks suspended in the air with thin rods connecting it all together in an odd but fascinating way. It would make a pretty cool sculpture if I could figure out how to replicate it in 3D. It was a start.

3D image from the internet. Note: the numbers and letters are mine.

I picked up some simple materials at the art store and set to work making a little model. With a ruler, I measured each block in the digital image and created a little Styrofoam version in the same proportions. Then I measured how far away they were from each other. With thin wire, I tried to position the blocks correctly to mimic the original image.

It didn't work. I tried a variety of ways to configure the blocks, but none of them created the effect I was hoping for. There was something odd about the spacing between the blocks in the picture that I could not capture in my real-life model. I gave the project up as a bad idea.

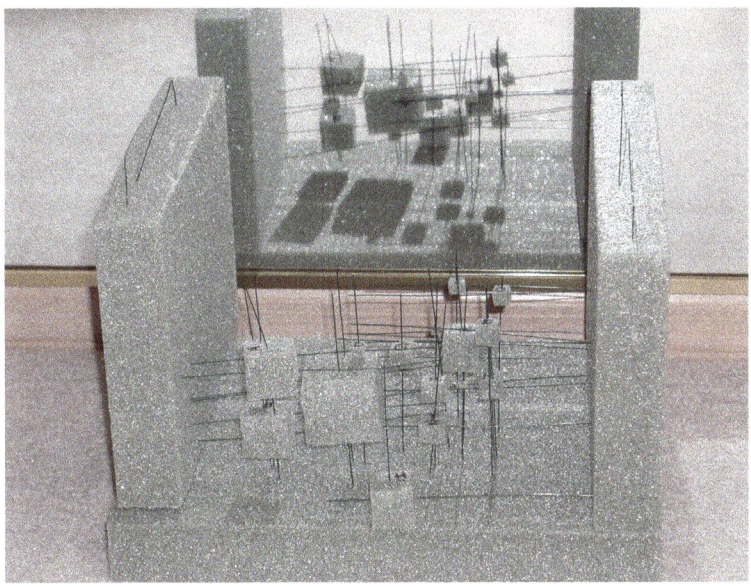

My attempt to replicate the internet image

The next morning, I stilled myself, listening for the quiet little voice inside, hoping to receive some suggestions. I heard:

Let's go shopping!

Shopping? Hmmm. Okay. Let's go. And off we went to Michaels. It was quite an adventure!

I got in the store, clueless as to what I was supposed to be looking for. Not to worry, though. I was given *plenty* of specifics! Inserted into my thought stream were very clear instructions.

> *Go down this aisle. Throw those Styrofoam balls into the basket. Three of this size, four of those, a couple of these too. Now, let's hit the paint aisle. Get a few shades of blue and also some white. Pick up a jar of that modeling paste. Now, let's get some dowels and that piece of wood (about 16" x 11"). Toss in a few brushes and a palette knife while we are at it. Okay, let's check out and go home.*

I set up a makeshift art studio on the dining room table and arranged the various items on it. I sat down and stilled my mind, opening myself to inspiration and instruction. I had no idea what to do with all the stuff I had just purchased.

Archangel Michael became present, pressing my temples in greeting and surrounding me with his powerful presence. He said:

> *Don't get frustrated with your sculpture.* (Meaning that first one with blocks.) *You were going about it the wrong way. You must be playful and childlike when you work on your projects. Make sure that is the energy you put into it.*
>
> *Start painting the spheres. Today we are painting in my colors.* (Michael's color is blue.) *Start with the darkest blue. Add the modeling paste to the lighter colors and just make swirls or whatever patterns come to you. Let me guide you. Just have fun painting.*

Remember you won't see the whole pattern until you are done. Stay out of your head.

Over the next few days, I worked on the sculpture. Each little ball had variations of blue and white. How they would come together into a cohesive sculpture eluded me, but somehow, I knew when each ball was painted just right.

After the balls were set to dry, I took pruning shears and cut the dowels at what seemed to me to be random lengths. Yet I had a gut sense again that each length was exactly right. Those I painted in the darkest blue.

I sanded the piece of wood smooth and painted it dark blue too. After it dried, I drilled holes into the wood in an apparently random pattern. I made a paper pattern of the hole placement, for reasons I could not fathom, but that is what came to me to do, so I did it, without question or needing to know the reason.

I glued a dowel into each sphere and then glued the other end into one of the drilled holes. It was the oddest experience I think I ever had. It was quite mysterious, and fun! I had no idea what I was doing, but it seemed to progress without a hitch. Each step was made clear to me in the moment when I needed to carry it out—and not a second before. Truly a trust walk!

When everything was glued together, I sat back and looked at what I/we created. Holy cow! There was a little universe sitting in front of me, and man, was it kicking off some energy, like an invisible fan giving off gentle waves of air that I could actually feel. I sat in front of it, resting my arms loosely around it, and soaked in the energies coming from this little powerhouse. I lost all track of time, and I felt only love and vastness coming from it. Merging with it, I too became love and vastness.

Atlantis, my first piece of art

I don't know how long I sat there, but eventually the moment dissipated. And still I didn't move. This little sculpture had transported me to a different way of feeling, of being, so expanded and immersed in pure love energy, I was taken way, way beyond words, beyond thought.

Even now, all these years later as I reread my journal entry and fill in the details, the moment, and the feeling, return to me in powerful, exquisite detail—every cell in me vibrating and completely alive. It's hard to pull away from it, even now.

How did I make that? Well, I didn't exactly. I *helped* create it. But I learned a lot in the process.

I learned that what I needed to know would come only one little piece at a time. I had to wait for the next instruction to bubble up and present itself before I could proceed.

I had to stay focused, curious, and open.

I had to stop my ego from trying to hurry the process up or trying to finish it the way *I* thought it should be. (Don't dog paddle!)

I had to suspend all expectations and simply allow it to unfold—to create itself, basically.

I was simply a tool for putting the pieces together. Perhaps the word "simply" is understated. It was amazing and a great honor to create with Michael guiding me.

Of all the art I've done since then, that little sculpture—made with Styrofoam, cheap acrylic paint, and dowels—is still my most treasured creation!

The next morning, I woke up feeling peaceful and put together. I mentally recited a very long list of everything I was grateful for, on and on and on. Then, when I finally took a mental "breath," I heard, in a voice with a smile in it:

Are you finished?

I smiled back—A beautiful, gentle reminder that conversations flow both ways. I wasn't petitioning or begging, but I *was* going on and on. Okay, message received. It was my turn to listen.

I was shown a hand, fingers spread, facing upward.

How many?

Of course, the obvious answer was five. Five fingers. Even a small child knows the answer. But no! The correct answer was nine. When counting the SPACES between the fingers, the answer was nine. It was a lesson in seeing things differently, to acknowledge that the spaces between were just as important as the fingers.

I had known that Atlantis' spheres were positioned in a certain formation, but apparently it was the spaces *between them* that generated that very palpable energy field. Archangel Michael said:

God works in the spaces between. Moves in the briefest of pauses in your mental flow to insert inspiration. Doesn't need an hour at church.

God moves in your life, all the time. It's up to you to open the channel to become aware of that. To communicate, to stop, and listen. And receive Spirit's huge inflowing of love, peace, and well being.

It's always there, moving through the cracks in your life. When you consciously open the door, floodgates, or mouse hole, it will flow happily and more powerfully to you. YOU control how much Grace you receive by how open you are to the Divine. It surrounds you in infinite supply. You walk and breathe and live in a soup of Love.

Wow. Just wow.

Chapter 10: Energy

I took Archangel Michael's earlier advice to heart—about being mindful of the energy I put into the creation process. I knew, better than anyone, that my mood and temper were not always the best. (I'm being kind to myself here.) I looked for a way to ensure that each sculpture would be created with the best energy I could give it.

Years before, my sister had shown me a book called *Hands of Light* by Barbara Brennan. I was mesmerized by the cover, which showed two hands held close together, palms out, with the most amazing light emitting from them. I borrowed the book, read it, and studied the illustrations inside. One showed the way people's energy manifests around them, affecting their posture and sometimes even the people around them.

I was especially drawn to a sketch of an energy healing session, with the healer and many other nonphysical Beings of Light surrounding the person, contributing to the healing session. Maybe that's how it was with Michael and me when we made that Atlantis sculpture.

I had even tried the experiment the author described in the beginning of the book, putting my hands together, then slowly pulling them apart and back together again, feeling a subtle tug and push between them. Prana. Energy. And I felt it. Anyone can do it. This force, or aura, was tangible if not visible.

Coincidentally, I noticed an advertisement for a Reiki healing session in the window of a local metaphysical bookshop—a shop that I *never* went in. The session sounded like the concepts I had read about in the book, and on a whim, out of curiosity, I signed up. I had absolutely no preconceptions about the session. All I knew was that it was some sort of energy healing session, and I wondered if it would be anything like the illustration I saw in the book.

Mind you, back then, all those years ago, I was in full corporate mode. That session did not jive or make sense with my life at all, but I did it anyway. Heck, it was just an hour of time on a Saturday afternoon.

Two people met me and asked me to lie down on a blanket on the floor in a quiet little back room. They started gently placing their hands on my head, feet, and then back. All this was new to me, and I really didn't expect anything to happen.

But then I felt a movement within my abdomen. It felt like worms wiggling around, and then I started crying, hard. Deep wrenching sobs. For no reason. It was strange, weird, but *real*. I don't cry easily, definitely not in front of other people. And there I was, sobbing for all I was worth, in front of two strangers.

Back to this storyline. I remembered the book and the energy session and wondered if Reiki might be the perfect solution to my mood problem. If I could learn to invoke that healing energy when I worked on the sculptures, maybe that energy, flowing from the Universe through my hands, would overrule my mind's general negativity and imbue the sculptures with something better than I could give. I found a class being held nearby and signed up.

It was fascinating, and we were encouraged to practice the techniques and hand positions on ourselves. I signed up for level 2 right away, which amped up the amount of energy that could flow through me to the sculptures.

Not only did I gain the knowledge I sought about Reiki, I also gained some amazing new friends who accepted this new emerging version of me. They encouraged my explorations and provided positive feedback and support.

One of those friends, Gay, was a massage therapist, and I started going to her for massages. Her extraordinary bodywork really helped me release a lot of tension as well as the lingering anxiety and negativity I had from my past corporate life.

Our massage sessions often had an amusing twist to them. She would tell me that she had planned to do thus-and-such on me, but my angels would butt in to *her* thought stream and instruct her very clearly to do *this* instead. I already knew my angels could be bossy, but she completely and unexpectedly confirmed it. And always, it turned out to be exactly what I needed at the time. How wonderful to be that lovingly looked after and cared for!

Chapter 11: The Art Evolves

The angels continued to encourage me to pursue art, telling me:

> *Your work will take on an intensity as you open to it. It will be one of your hallmarks. Just allow the colors and energies to flow from your hands. Bless it as you create it. Infuse love into its being as each will have an essence, a consciousness of sorts.*
>
> *The more you approach your work with the joy and innocence of a child, the more powerful the work will become. You are not a Picasso. Picasso was Picasso. You are you, and the work that flows through you is blessed, holy, and unique to your energies. Never judge it. Just love it intensely and offer it humbly to the world to help make others smile and find their joy and playfulness.*

Maybe the angels were helping me to redirect the intense ambition I had during my corporate life. I really can't say, but their encouragement definitely ignited and honed the focus I gave to creating from that point on.

Over time, the sculptures evolved. I incorporated better materials, such as exotic wood bases instead of pine, brass or copper rods instead of dowels, and hardwood spheres instead of Styrofoam. I even included crystals, feathers, and other natural materials. I called them "Tabletop Universes" because they looked like tiny groupings of stars.

It quickly became apparent that each sculpture was a true collaboration. A beautiful, unseen presence guided me with each creation. Archangel Michael only worked with me on the first piece. After that, it felt like many different Light Beings lined up to take their turn creating with me. My role was to take the concepts they communicated and make them visible and tangible in our world.

I was told that each Tabletop Universe possessed a unique energy signature and purpose. Some were intended to heal emotions, some to connect us to the earth, etc. Creating became a little easier as I gained proficiency in listening to inner guidance and acting on the instructions given. When I questioned the instructions or chose to do something the way I wanted to do it, the flow stopped abruptly and immediately. I quickly learned to set ego and opinion aside when the creative juices were flowing.

It was a far cry from life in the corporate world. Just a few months before, I would never have imagined myself doing any of this. One suggestion given, because I asked for guidance, set me on a new trajectory for my life. It was a very fulfilling time for me. Finally on a clear path, I created many little Tabletop Universes.

I was deeply content creating the sculptures, learning so many new things and experiencing their unique energies. This truly was living. It was a gift of time and circumstance.

And yet, the needs of the "real" world lurked and niggled at me. My real-world anxiety, which had become a subterranean current in my thoughts, resurfaced. What was I doing? I still was not generating any income. Responsibility to my family and guilt that I wasn't contributing weighed heavily on me.

Some of my Tabletop Universes

One particular day started out great. I felt full of love and peace and balance, but I lost it somewhere along the way. I was blocked at all turns. My phone was not working, my printer was not working, my car was not working, and I had no income in sight.

My sister said, "What you are trying to do is too hard. Just go get a job!"

But I just couldn't. I couldn't explain it, but every bone in my body, every nerve and fiber within me rebelled at the thought. I literally got nauseous when I considered it. Maybe this was the illogical path of the heart that the angels told me about.

Fear and anxiety overwhelmed me. Where was all this leading me? Was I just fooling myself with all this spiritual art jazz? In desperation, I threw a big hissy fit at the angels, screaming, "I KNOW I AM CAUSING THESE BLOCKS BUT NOT WHY OR HOW! PLEASE HELP ME! I ASK FOR THINGS TO START TO CHANGE *TODAY*!!"

I put the latest sculptures in the car, resolving to have them placed in a gallery or restaurant or store or somewhere before I returned home. If I still had them all at the end of the day, I vowed to give up on the art stuff and apply to the local grocery store for a cashier position the very next day.

I stopped at a gallery in a nearby town. Not only did they take my work, but they also wanted more pieces! It felt like a good "opening" place, but just a stepping stone. The owners were older folks, low energy, but local and welcoming. But I got placed! Hallelujah! I thanked the angels for their speedy response to my call for help! Clearly, I was supposed to stay focused on the artwork and release the "real" world anxieties once again.

I continued to create more pieces over time, but I began to feel the need to work on a larger scale. The book recommended to me by Hazel, the sound healer I met in Washington State, *Christ Power and the Earth Goddess*, introduced me to sacred geometry and how it is incorporated in all the sacred sites around the world, including Stonehenge. I can't recall exactly why I decided to recreate the Sarsen Circle, which is a part of the Stonehenge complex, but that became my next project.

I researched the structure and made some calculations to determine the scale needed for this new venture. I also had to find a new medium to create it and learn how to work with that. I chose concrete because of its ability to withstand the elements. My memory of the original angelic message of creating "beauty on a grand scale" that might be placed outdoors influenced those choices.

Because working with concrete in the dining room was not a good idea, I moved my workspace into the garage. We had a six-car garage at the time and only two cars. There was plenty of room.

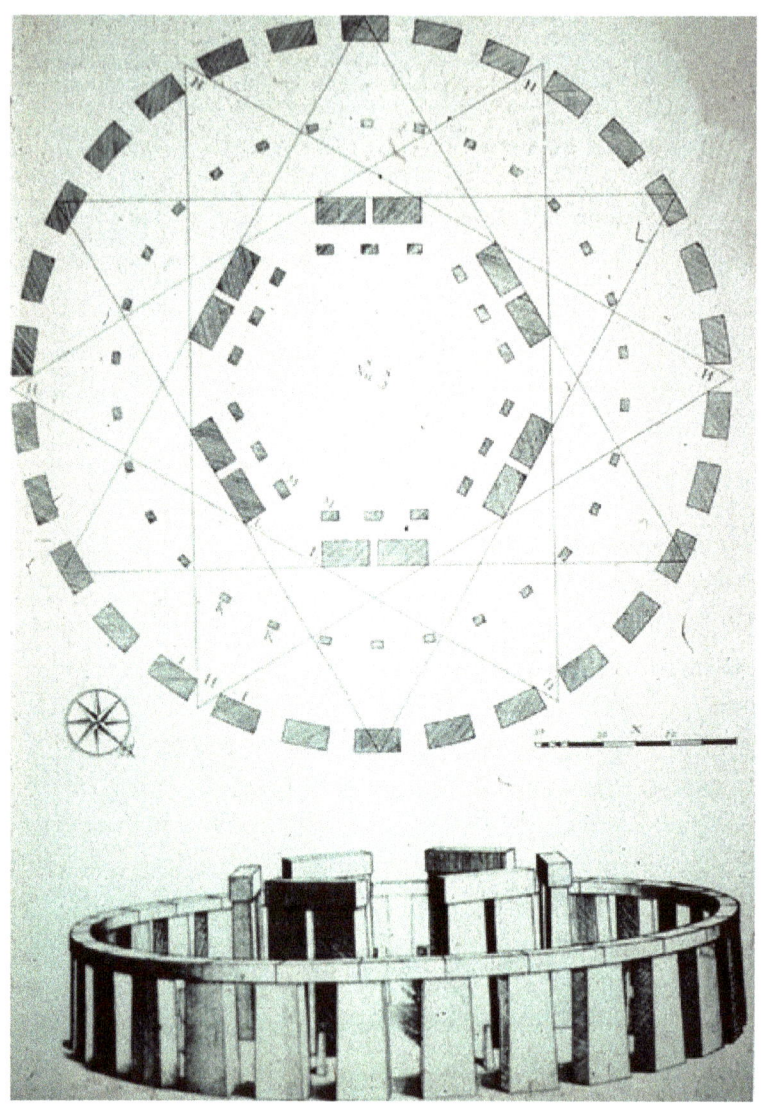

Diagram of the Sarsen Circle (the outer rings)
of Stonehenge

The sculpture took months to finish. The stones and capstones all connected together to form a circle about six feet in diameter and about ten inches high. It had sixty pieces in all—thirty pillars and thirty capstones.

At first, I built the sculpture to rest on the ground, with wires protruding out of the bottom of each stone to anchor them into the ground. I set it up in my yard and invited Gay over. We took turns sitting inside the circle and agreed that it facilitated quicker and deeper meditation.

Me meditating within the Stonehenge sculpture

Then I received another nudge to build a base structure so that the sculpture could be set up indoors or on pavement. So back to the garage I went. This time I used white concrete.

The interesting and curious part of this long, tedious process was the symbols that came to me to incorporate into the base structure. It started one morning over a cup of coffee. I saw a symbol in my mind. Just one. I took a sketch pad and drew what I saw.

Later, I incorporated the symbol in black to the inside of the block being fashioned that day. That happened nine more times over the course of the base's construction. Ten different symbols came clearly to me, exactly when needed and were equally spaced around the circle.

These symbols were not from any language I knew of or could find online. I still have no idea where they come from. I just knew they needed to be part of the sculpture and that they represented a chant.

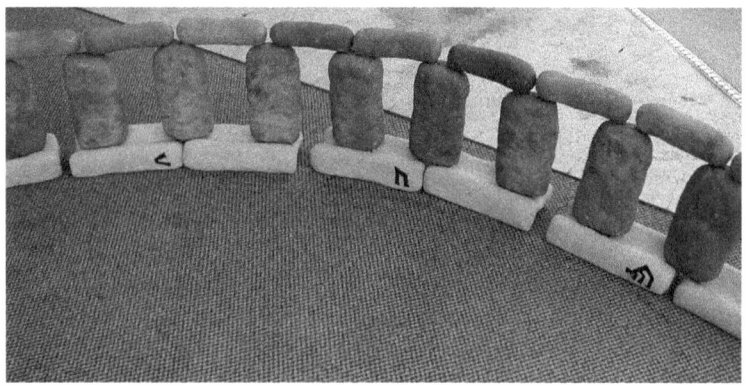

Some of the symbols incorporated into the base of the Stonehenge sculpture

When the base was complete, I was instructed to create one last element, which would be separate from the circle. It was to be an activation device, made of copper, and placed within a small concrete base.

Stonehenge sculpture activation device

I set up the entire circle on my back patio on a circle of canvas I had made for the purpose. Around the outer perimeter of the canvas I had added twelve Flower of Life symbols that represented life and oneness. I had become aware of it through my research on sacred geometry and knew that it needed to be part of the overall sculpture.

I sat inside the completed circle and closed my eyes. In my mind's eye, I saw each of the sculpture's symbols again. To my surprise, I heard a sound that went with each symbol. It was very similar to seeing the letter A and then hearing what an A sounds like in English.

Repeating the chant a few times, I found my consciousness in a very different place. My body was still sitting within the circle, but my awareness was at Machu Picchu. I'd never been there, but I'd seen photographs of the place, so I knew where I was. But I was inside someplace not normally accessible as a tourist—down inside a building with dark water, like a well, nearby.

Profound silence. Ancient beyond ancient. Holy. Writing this I am transported back there again. Time slips and suspends. I am connected to that vast and endless energy of love and peace once again, like how I felt when I finished that first sculpture with Michael. My heart stretched its boundaries from being filled so full of this love. It even ached a little, like your stomach does when you have eaten too much Thanksgiving dinner.

Eventually my awareness returned, mostly, to the circle. I relaxed for the rest of the day. Wow. Who knew that a collection of concrete shapes could cause such an experience?

I invited several friends over to see what they might experience from it. It would either confirm my experience, or not. It turned into quite an unusual party. In my corporate days, parties involved a lot of alcohol, food, and music. This time everyone brought interesting, mostly healthy food. I made a spiced tea.

One of my friends brought all her crystal singing bowls and lined them up out in the lanai. As the sun slipped below the horizon and the sky turned to fire, she played them. Pure powerful tones filled the air, clearing our minds and bodies of unnecessary thoughts and stress. Magical.

Then we moved to the stone circle. We each stood on one of the Flower of Life symbols. Huh. More people were expected, but only twelve came. Perfect. Each of us took a turn inside the circle. Each person's experience was different but profound. It was a truly remarkable evening.

The completed Stonehenge sculpture and activation rod

A few months later, I had my first show at the gallery and included both Stonehenge and the Tabletop Universes.

I received a good response from the people who came to the opening. As unbelievable as it would have seemed not so long ago in my corporate life, here I was having an art show in a gallery. I even sold my first sculpture, which helped me start accepting myself as an artist. It might take a while, but art seemed to be the way forward for me.

Stonehenge and Tabletop Universes at my first art show

I believed that I could support myself financially doing my soul's work, whatever that was (rather than getting a traditional job). I thought it was to be my art and teaching, but I sensed that might not be quite right. There could be something else. I asked for guidance:

> *Open to the happy surprises and amazing situations that are coming your way. You are very much loved and honored. Many have lined up to help you. Maybe too many! Be at peace. Stay centered and balanced. Trust that you will be perfectly delivered to the far shore.*
>
> *Don't fret over the details and worries of your life. They will sort themselves out most quickly if you stop chewing on them. Remember to stay unattached to people, places, situations, and outcomes. It will be more joyful to you if you allow a little fun and adventure to come into your life. The more you relax, play, and seek out the things that energize you, the easier you make it for us to deliver you where you need to be and bring you what you need.*

Fears put to rest once again by this advice, I continued with even more conviction to produce sculptures, rather than look for a job. I truly felt that by following this path I would be okay—even if it looked crazy to everyone around me. All this put a strain on my marriage and our finances, but I stayed committed.

The next project was pretty ambitious. I returned to the very first sculpture, Michael's *Atlantis*, and I imagined it biggie-sized and installed outside for people to walk through, just like the angels had originally said. If it emitted a similar energy as the original, it could be quite a remarkable experience—a true healing force for people.

More calculations were needed. Up-scaling the little sculpture by a factor of seven seemed to be the right number. The finished work would take up the size of a typical room, maybe a little more. I figured out what materials to use and where to find them or get them fabricated. Safety and weather resistance were key factors I used to evaluate my options.

It turned out that in order to complete the plan I needed that little paper pattern of hole placement from the original Atlantis sculpture after all. Everything I needed was always provided for, often long before I even needed it. That was another lesson in not questioning the little suggestions that came, especially the strange ones. Everything eventually gets used.

It was a good thing I had a big garage. I needed it for all the materials and supplies I collected for the project. Concrete is extremely alkaline, and it can burn skin, just like acid. Therefore, I took many precautions. I wore long-sleeved work shirts, old jeans, and sturdy shoes for standing for hours on the hard concrete garage floor. I wore goggles to protect my eyes and thick plastic gloves.

Anything I needed from the house—phone, water, snacks, music—I had to get ready before I started. Mind you, this all happened in the middle of a Florida summer. The garage was often well over 100 degrees, and I was in all my protective garb. It was quite the sweat fest! Sometimes the goggles got so fogged up I had to take them off for a while.

Work proceeded slowly, but I kept at it. To while away the hours, I played music CDs that I could put on repeat all day because concrete-covered hands played havoc on a CD player. I also listened to several audio series, gaining knowledge on interesting topics as I slowly built each sphere.

Spending all those long hours in the garage led me to develop a habit of staying in touch with the angels off and on all day in a sort of running conversation. I knew I was always surrounded by them, and because we were friends, I talked to them that way. They could be playful or sarcastic and opinionated, but their advice was always right.

It was nice to know that they were looking out for me, helping me, challenging me, teaching me. They were the toughest teachers I have ever had, never accepting less than my best effort, never cutting me a break until I got the lesson and made the internal shift of attitude or perception.

The painting, concrete, and healing experiences showed me that together we formed a cohesive team. We had the same goal, but we played different roles to achieve it, like that image in *Hands of Light* that so fascinated me years before with the unseen members of the healing team surrounding and assisting the person being healed.

Or like a sports team. There's the coach who understands the game and knows the team members better than they know themselves. The coach knows the goals and the strategy to achieve them and knows how to best utilize each player. Each player has a specific role and function.

My "team" members were harder to see than me, but the results of their efforts were always unmistakable, taking care of the background details, orchestrating synchronicities, coincidences, and opportunities. Some shouted directions into my stubborn head. Meanwhile, I took the ball into the end zone, filled water bottles, or did whatever I was asked to do in the moment—like go get PEZ candy dispensers.

There was usually a gang of them with me. They had no specific personalities. They were just a group of loving, wise Beings hanging out with me.

I initially thought of the team as Me in the middle and them orbiting around me. Then it occurred to me that I was *part* of the team, *not* in the center. No one was in the center, except maybe the Coach.

With that flash of insight, the way I looked at my life completely changed. It was no longer about my purpose. The *entire* team had a *shared* purpose. And the Coach knew what it was. It was best to turn to him (for me the Coach was male for whatever reason) for the next play.

I stopped seeking direction from specific angels and instead communicated with the Team. Sometimes Michael still visited with me, but the need to chat with individual angelic personalities was no longer important.

I did my best to stay focused on my ambitious project, but I was faced with a new challenge. My husband was offered a promotion, which meant moving out of state and putting the house up for sale. Could I get the project done before my workspace was gone?

The message I kept getting was to focus on the work before me, stay in the energy of love and compassion, and release negativity, old beliefs, and anger.

Chapter 12: Letting Go

Several years after I was downsized, things came to head between my husband and me. Ever since I'd stopped working, we had slowly grown apart. He had been more than patient with me. He never pressured me to get a job. But my new life did not interest him in the least, and I was not thrilled to hear about his very corporate days and challenges.

I also was not thrilled to move back north, closer to the headquarters of the company that let me go. I liked the Florida sunshine, heat, and lack of winter. I was not ready to stop what I was doing either. Being both conflict-averse, we just quietly drifted apart.

But the upcoming relocation forced me to do some deep soul searching and to make a choice. Option one was to abandon all the art and the avant-garde way of living that I'd gotten used to and become "socially acceptable" again.

Option two was to choose to live my odd but satisfying and interesting life, to stand up for myself, stand against my tribe, my family and friends, and walk away from my old life, my husband and family. I might lose their support and respect and become shunned. Be completely on my own. Could I do it? Could I *not* do it? The choice was devastating to contemplate.

A gift of synchronicity came to me as I wrestled with this terrifying choice. I watched a *Star Trek: Next Gener-*

ation episode that gave me exactly what I needed at that moment. The young boy Wesley had a vision quest (from a Native American tradition) and broke away from his tribal/familial expectations in order to follow an unusual and amazing opportunity. It was exactly, coincidentally, shown to me at this moment in my life. And it was in lock-step with what I had been reading about the fourth chakra from one of Carolyn Myss's books. She wrote, "To follow your path, you must break away from 'tribal' (societal) expectations."

Finally, I told my husband that I was not going to move north with him. He was angry and hurt. Life, as I had known it, was over. I didn't know where my life was headed, but now I knew where it was not.

Family from both sides were upset and couldn't understand. I never wanted to hurt my husband, or them. I don't even know that I could have explained it to them in a way they would accept. I drifted away from the scorn and judgments, walked away from my tribe.

In the end, the house sold long before I was done with the project. I had put in well over 100 hours, and it would probably have needed another 400 or more just to cover the balls with concrete. In addition, the constant exposure to the concrete ate my hands up. Even through protective hand cream and *two* pairs of heavy gloves, the alkalinity still came through. By the time I had to stop, every finger was covered in Band-Aids to soak up the spontaneous bleeding that even small hand movements caused. I don't think I could have continued even if I wanted to. I boxed up the balls, supplies, and equipment.

And I boxed up a big chapter of my life. Confused, frustrated, and feeling extremely fragile, the last molecules of my old life dissolved into a puddle of goo.

We will take you down to nothing before we let you back up.

The angels weren't lying. Like the caterpillar within the chrysalis, the structure of my life had melted down all around me. All the beliefs I grew up with and thought were true were tested and shattered. And yet, during this time of personal demolition, I couldn't have done anything differently. Finding a job was impossible. Every cell in my being rebelled, and even when I sent resumes out by the dozens, not one, *not one,* resulted in even a call back.

Chapter 13: A New Home

I moved into a room rented to me by my friend Patty. I put the balls of concrete in storage—along with most of the rest of my belongings. I went from knocking around a 3,000-square-foot house with a pool and six-car garage, mostly by myself, to having a 10-by-10-foot room to call my own. Only the barest of essentials came with me. Everything else was piled away in a U-Haul storage locker. My life was compressed down to practically nothing.

I had no space to create—at least not like I had before. I could use Patty's dining room table, but I had to put everything away at the end of each session. I could make no drips or spills. Using concrete was out of the question. Sanding wood was out of the question.

Shortly after I moved in, I landed a consulting job in the middle of rural Ohio. I travelled back and forth on the weekends and stayed in a Hampton Inn during the week. To fill the long quiet evenings, I started to make little pictures on paper, which was easily done in a hotel room and taken home at the end of the week.

It was a completely new way to create, shifting from large concrete spheres to sheets of paper. I was doing my best to adapt to the world I found myself in. Balancing working-me with spiritually creative-me, turned out to be less difficult than I thought, once I learned to leave work at work. That was new too, not obsessing over the work when I left for the day.

What showed up on the paper were symbols unlike anything I'd seen before, yet reminiscent of the ones on "Stonehenge's" base. They felt like phrases, or paragraphs, but I couldn't decipher them. I just made them. Maybe more accurately, they flowed onto the paper through my hands. Like taking dictation.

Symbols painted while consulting in Ohio

I started calling myself an innocent savant, mostly in jest. I was making symbols that clearly were important and had something to say, but I was clueless as to their meaning or purpose. But this was something I was getting used to—listening and acting on the instructions, without being privy to or understanding the reason or purpose.

After the consulting assignment ended and I was back in Florida full time, the "hotel" symbol paintings evolved into more complex paintings on canvas. I experimented with various types of paint and found acrylics to my liking. For me, oil paint took too long to dry, and the odor was unpleasant in the house. I also discovered some very interesting fabric paint (Lumiere by Jacquard) with beautiful metallic colors that shift in the light like a hologram. They were easy to work with, easy to clean up, and work well with any other acrylics or mediums I wished to play with.

My old friend the black swan showed up unexpectedly in one of my very early paintings. I was working on a cosmic theme, with deep space, stars, and a planet. It was reminiscent of the Tabletop Universes, except the paint spilled. While working through the "mistake," the image of a black swan emerged instead, floating through the cosmos, apparently on its way to who knows where. That was an important lesson from Spirit, to take what seems to be a mistake and find the hidden perfection within it.

"Black Swan Journeys"

I loved painting circles and spheres. Maybe I felt the way Black Elk, the famous Lakota medicine man, felt. I read a quote of his that rang so true for me.

The power of the world always works in circles, and everything tries to be round. The sky is round, and I have heard that the earth is round like a ball and so are all the stars. The wind, in its greatest power, whirls. Birds make their nests in circles, for theirs is the same religion as ours. Even the seasons form a great circle in their changing and always come back again to where they were. The life of a man is a circle from childhood to childhood, and so it is in everything where power moves.

"Creation"

Occasionally, I was nudged to un-create or over-paint an area on the canvas. Each time, I hesitated. What was the point of spending time, applying all that paint, just to take it all off again? Maybe I wasn't listening closely enough in the first place. Or maybe my ego got involved and was directing the work, and for that it had to be removed? Or maybe the un-creating was simply a little pop quiz from the Universe to see if I would do as nudged, without argument. Could I trust the process?

Over time, I learned to take the un-create / re-create process in stride, accepting that when this happened, the painting was ready to transform into something better.

Just like life, I realized. Each of us goes through un-creation, decomposition, and then re-birth, over and over throughout our lives.

Experiencing the same cycle while painting, learning to trust it, and seeing the positive results each time made it a little less scary in life. Trust the process ...

It is customary for artists to sign their creations. I found it uncomfortable, perhaps even unethical, to sign my name to the paintings and sculptures I was making. It seemed to me that I was just an administrative assistant, so to speak. There was someone, or some Being, much greater than I, directing the whole affair, and I felt that they should get the credit.

I chewed on the whole co-creation concept for a long time. Finally, a solution presented itself to me. In medita-tion, a symbol came into my mind's eye. I wrote it down, a few times, to make sure I got it right, then asked what it represented. Apparently, it represented me—an energetic signature perhaps. But also, like Stonehenge's symbols, it had an associated sound. The symbol was pronounced "AH – nee – KA" and it meant "Beloved Little Daughter of RA." Well, I was still unclear what that meant exactly, but it felt like something appropriate to sign my creations with.

Symbolic signature of AhneeKA

Chapter 14: Life Expands

I thought I would be staying at Patty's for just a few months, but it turned out to be two years. I learned to manage my life in a small space. We had many fun adventures, including going to my first sweat lodge and a drum circle. She also invited me to attend classes with her from a professor who taught mediumship. Although I did learn how to connect with people who passed over, it definitely was not my cup of tea.

However, during one class he taught us how to connect, in a much deeper way than Reiki did, to the powerful flow of life force all around us, for the purpose of providing energetic/spiritual healing for another. It was an amazing experience. There was no touching, or running energy intentionally, as in a Reiki session. Instead, we were simply to open ourselves fully to Spirit, invite it to flow through us to help the person we were working with.

At the end of class, the teacher asked three of us at a time to come to the front of the classroom and stand behind three other students to demonstrate the techniques we had just learned.

As instructed, I stretched my arms out straight, along either side of the person's head in front of me, about eight inches away from either ear, hands facing toward each other. Closing my eyes, tucking my ego into my back pocket, I opened myself to Spirit.

I felt a huge flow of energy move through me, causing my arms to open wide, out to the side, like a T. I felt like I was embracing the whole room. My back arched of its own accord, heart opened, head tilted back, like I was about to fly. I felt the energy move out, full force, from my heart. It felt to me like a gale wind whipping through the room. After a few intense seconds, I opened my eyes and saw that some of the other students who had been standing at the back of the room were now pushed back against the wall. By the energy?

I looked over at the teacher for his read on what just happened. His eyes were opened in surprise and nodded to me. Yes, that really just happened. Later, he told me that I had a unique gift for healing and warned me not to be too modest or I could thwart it.

My challenge then was to embrace this ability without getting into ego. A message I had received just the day before said, "Just do it and stop worrying so much". Between these two back-to-back messages, I committed to continuing to learn and practice energetic healing.

I learned about crystals and how they can facilitate healing. Same with essential oils. I acquired a Tibetan bowl and Tingsha bells, a rattle, Australian rain stick, a djembe, and of course my native drum, Speaker. I also took a lomilomi class, learning the art of weaving mind, body, and spirit through that particular massage methodology. It was all wonderful.

Over time, I learned how to use those various tools in healing sessions. Tuning in for guidance before and during a session, I intuitively saw how to proceed, and when, if, and how to use any of the modalities I had learned.

Interestingly, the process for healing was very much the same as painting. Becoming still inside, opening to

Spirit, following the instructions. Staying out of my head, staying in my heart. Letting go of any expectations for the process, or the outcome. Trusting that what needed to happen, would happen.

It became clear to me that my healing ability was best used for emotional and spiritual support. I enjoyed offering the sessions and received positive feedback from the people I worked on.

I asked Spirit to help me increase my capacity to love unconditionally. Spirit told me that in order to do this I also needed to increase my capacity to *receive* love unconditionally. If I could do this, it would significantly increase the effectiveness of my work.

———

For many months, I had heard the question in my mind:

"Can you feel our love?"

And the answer had always been, and still was, no, but I wanted to. I had a block somewhere inside me that needed to be released. I didn't know whether I should seek to find the source of the blockage or work on filling my heart with gratitude to blast it open from there. All I knew was that there was actual physical discomfort around my heart and solar plexus.

One day, I dropped into a meditative state, entering my heart from behind, and went to a grove of trees. It was my special place to have conversations with my teachers. It was a smallish circular grove, maybe twenty feet in diameter, with nicely trimmed grass in the center, three rather large stones clustered together to the right, and encircled by a lovely stand of slender birch-like trees.

Kahiki (a large Polynesian guide I had acquired recently) showed up, and gave me a big hug. He entered the grove like it was my living room. "Nice place, eh?" was the sense I got as he looked around. He walked over to a stream that I had never noticed before. He said it *wasn't* there before, but it needed to be there today. It was a nice babbling brook with soft grassy banks of spring grass and wildflowers.

Next came three Native American guides. Suddenly, it felt like a party, and guests were starting to arrive. I greeted the Grandfather elder of the Native Americans. He told me that he had been with me a long time—that the face I created on the scratchboard back in high school art class had been him. I knew him even back then at some unconscious level!

Thinking back, I remember feeling compelled to create that image and was pleasantly surprised when it turned out as good as it did, not being much of an artist then. He handed me a piece of pipestone, saying that it bound us together, then walked away, looking for a smoke.

I recognized the young native boy who walked up to me next. I saw him, or someone like him, in a *National Geographic* magazine several years back. I was captivated by the photograph of his face in the magazine the moment I saw it. I felt like I knew him well from another place and time. Maybe because he's one of my guides? He had such clear eyes, with ancient wisdom and compassion shining from them, which is rare for one so young. He was from South America, from the tribe in the clouds who see themselves as caretakers of the planet.

I always felt that this tribe, this boy, had such a purity about them. Just looking at that picture and reading the article made me want to take better care of the planet too. And now, here he was in my special grove! I was delighted to see him here. He greeted me quietly, then wandered off to join the others.

Finally, I focused on the young native man before me. I had trouble seeing his face, like it wouldn't quite come into focus. I saw his black hair hanging just above his shoulders, and he said to me:

You know me.

And I did. He had been my son, about fourteen, in another life, the one who died on the Trail of Tears. I felt this and started to cry. I loved this boy so much. Strong feelings from that lifetime erupted inside me. It was not right that he should die, that we should be forced to march in the winter. It was not right. He told me to let it go. It was as it needed to be, so we could be reunited now in joy. He said that he has watched over me ever since—for many lifetimes.

I felt the truth of his words. Through my tears, I hugged him tightly and then let him move on to join the rest of my growing party.

I saw them over by the stream, starting a drum circle. I became aware of the land and trees in that grove, every sense amplified. The many shades of green were intense and vibrant. The pulse of life in the grove was palpable, pressing on me, in me, supporting me, loving me. The trees, the rocks, the grass. Everything I'd taken for granted in this sacred grove was now in sharp relief, and I felt our deep connection.

A golden eagle flew to a branch near me, looking me in the eye. Fierce, strong, wise. He said that I had the spirit of an eagle too. Needing the connection of the land, but living for the flight, partnering with the wind, soaring on the unseen. I lived between two worlds, in complete harmony with both.

Next to arrive was a whole caravan of angels. They all came at once, laughing and chatting amongst themselves as they approached the grove. I welcomed them in. There were so many, and they greeted me with big hugs. These apparently were the party angels, bringing food and drink for everyone. Every detail of the party was handled, and they went bustling off to join the others.

Then I sensed a tall single man at the entrance, wearing a white cloak with a hood, sort of like Gandalf in *Lord of the Rings*. But when he pushed his hood back, I saw that it was Jesus. He was immediately recognizable to me, looking the same as when I had walked the beach with Him as a teen. Early thirties, cream colored robe, shoulder length brown hair and beard.

Very quietly, in His beautiful baritone voice, He asked for permission to enter my grove, to come into my heart. I felt a hesitation. I still carried a smolder of anger toward him from that incident with the scumbag at the church as a teen, even though I *knew* it was not His fault. My teen self had felt betrayed, unprotected, and those feelings were still stuck somewhere inside me.

Being polite and a people pleaser, though, I said of course! But He didn't move. He said it couldn't be done like that, that I really had to want Him to come in. He continued to stand there, looking at me while I sorted this out. What was the right response to get Him to come in? For me to *want* Him to come in?

Honestly, Jesus hadn't really been in my thoughts for many years. I could deal with angels, my Team, and God, but I had rather snubbed Jesus during my spiritual awakening. The hurt and resentment I carried cut Him off from me.

But there He stood, outside my grove, sort of forcing the issue. I took a breath and looked into His eyes. In that moment, my heart released and opened, and my forgiveness was instantaneous, easy, complete.

Suddenly, I wanted to rewind the tape and start this encounter over. Again, I saw Him walking up the path toward the grove, and this time I ran out, down the path to meet Him even before He got close to the entrance. I threw my arms around Him in a big bear hug, *so* happy to see Him, so very happy He was there!

He started laughing and pulled out a bottle of wine from His robes. Of course! What else? How perfect. I dragged Him into the grove, so happy! His light shone everywhere in the grove. The life force and love that I had felt before from the trees and the land just amped up many many times.

We walked over and joined the party. I started to sit down, but instead the gaggle of angels all insisted that they take care of me. One brushed my hair, one massaged my shoulders, one worked on my nails and chatted like a gal from the Bronx. (*Oh, honey! You would not believe...!*). Gum and everything.

It felt nice to be pampered, to be surrounded by so many friends. Then Jesus knelt down and started to wash my feet. This pushed my buttons. I was *not* worthy of this. I should be washing His! He looked me in the eye and showed me how I have ministered to others, and now, similarly, He was ministering to me. I struggled with this.

Then He stepped into His power and said, *Hey, washing feet is nothing compared to all that I went through leading up to, and through, the events at the cross. Please don't make all that be in vain. It was not easy to pass through all the humiliation, the betrayal, the torture, and pain. Not easy at all, but it was my choice to take on the energy of all people, places and time.*

In that moment His capacity to love, to forgive, blew open an entirely new understanding within me what love truly is. It really *was* unhelpful for me to anchor old energy. It counteracted all that He achieved. It was better to jump into those waves of love, the endless ocean of love, of personal potentiality. The expanding consciousness of God.

What a party!

Chapter 15: Expansion

Patty challenged me to paint bigger, to open myself to much larger expressions than I had been working on to that point. That was one of her greatest gifts—to open me up to bigger ... more ... whether it was painting or healing work or sweat lodges. She invited me to paint a mural in her downstairs bathroom. It was wild and colorful, with a watery theme and patterns that flowed across all four walls.

Details of bathroom mural

Details of bathroom mural

As I became comfortable with "bigger," I found that I needed a larger workspace. I rented an office and set up my studio space within it. I painted one wall of the office in another flowing colorful mural. I distinctly remember getting stuck on one section, working on it over and over. My mind and ego had gotten in the middle of things, deciding the image should look like *this*. Spirit let me go round and round and round until finally I realized what I had done. When I released the need to make it *my* way and opened to inspiration, the mural finished easily and quickly. Lesson learned, again.

Detail of mural in my office studio

One day, I was in the studio working on a commission for a client. I received a clear suggestion to ask the receptionist to take a few photos of me while I painted. That sounded like a great idea because I was in the process of updating my website and marketing materials.

I have never liked my photo taken so I asked her to catch me in the zone of my creativity, rather than posing for a shot. She made a comment about blurry hands, but I didn't give it much thought because I wanted to keep painting.

Later that evening, I looked at the photos. I was totally astounded at what I saw. There were two left hands painting. Perhaps it was the effect of the flash, but all the other details of the image were crisp. I'd like to think that she captured the essence of Spirit who always worked with me when I painted. One hand mine, one hand Spirit's.

Painting with Spirit

Regardless of how the image happened, I treasured it for truly reflecting my creative process—creating beauty in complete harmony, and collaboration, with Spirit.

It had been a long process to learn to let go of control and trust that each painting would be perfect in the end, especially when a particular color or brushstroke seemed wrong but turned out just right.

Just like my life. I was learning to let go, knowing my life was being created perfectly each moment, even in those moments and circumstances that felt so wrong. Focusing on the distant horizon with happy anticipation increased the probability of best potentials happening. Without defining or putting rules or conditions on it. Just attracting it to me through love, curiosity, and happy anticipation. Like a child. Simple joy.

Oh, my. How long had I been encouraged to become like a child? The team once told me that I could only pass through to the next stage of my life in the energy of a child.

It had taken so long for me to grow young again, to set aside the accumulated disappointment, anger, and frustration and catch a glimpse of relaxed, joyful Kathy again. I knew there were many more thorns, prickles, and weeds still to clear out, but I'd at least caught a glimpse! I had felt it. Someday, with continued practice, it might become my default state—to be happily curious about the fun adventures yet to come.

Chapter 16: Working with Jesus

One night I had a vivid dream of many people suing me for wrongs they thought I did to them. I almost never remembered my dreams, but because this one was so vivid I took it as a message that I had an issue to address.

The day before, I had been upset with someone for rescheduling a meeting with me, again. She had done this several times. It was a possible opportunity to do some consulting and earn some income, so I was hopeful and ready to talk about the details. Instead, after blowing me off for two weeks, she gave the job to someone else—with no explanation.

I felt many things in that moment, all overlapping and amplifying each other. Not surprisingly, anger and frustration dominated.

Once I realized how much anger I was holding toward her, I tried the mantra I had learned. "Could I let it go? Would I let it go? Will I let it go?" But I just couldn't.

I was stuck in a dark place of my own making, but after waking up with that intimidating litigation dream still swirling in my mind, I asked Jesus to help me work it out.

Going into meditation, I found my inner self walking down an old, well-worn path with moss growing between the bricks, making a velvety cushion for my feet. On either side were low bushes with taller shrubs and bigger trees further back, with a carpet of pretty wildflowers.

The light was softly diffused by the overhead leaves. It was a cozy, welcoming place.

Up ahead, I noticed a man walking down the path ahead of me, and then I realized it was Jesus. He stopped and waited for me to catch up. I walked toward Him, and then, almost like He wasn't there, I walked *into* Him. I slipped into His body from behind, like we were shadows, smooth and easy.

Jesus instructed me to deepen the merge, step by step, by repeating the following sentences, with a few slow, deep breaths between each one to imagine and really feel what the sentence was describing,

> *I see with Your eyes.*
> *I hear with Your ears.*
> *I speak with Your mouth.*
> *My words are Your words.*
> *My thoughts are Your thoughts.*
> *My hands are Your hands.*
> *I feel what You feel.*

It was a remarkable experience. I truly could see through His eyes and experience each of the other sensations in the litany. The more I followed His instructions, the more I felt a little light-headed. He said it was just me getting used to His higher vibration. In the future, I would not notice it as much.

Once the merge was completed, Jesus told me,

> *You cannot forgive when you don't have love in your heart. Forgiveness requires that you send love energy directly from there in a strong flow to the object of unforgiveness. Let that flow wash away all the negativity, cleanse their auras, remove the karma between you.*

To truly forgive is a very powerful act of love. It is NOT a sense of "whatever!" It is washing away their sins, our sins, your sins, which, by the way, simply means stepping off the path, being out of the flow.

So, the first step in forgiveness is to fill yourself so full of love that it naturally flows outward to others. It is much easier to flow love out to the world in general, much more challenging to direct and focus the love on someone you are upset with.

First, take deep, centering, grounding breaths. Then cleanse your energy body of obstructions. Illuminate on the inhale, eliminate on the exhale.

I got a visual of my energy body like very long hair, with me gently brushing and combing all the tangles out.

Gather all your power back to yourself, with the sun over your head, calling back, reordering, cleansing, and returning it to your body through the crown of the head.

I noticed that my thoughts began to distract me away from my task. The ego wanted to hold on to my angry feelings and was uninterested in the heart's desire to release them. I returned again and again to my breathing, clearing thoughts, gathering stray power.

Jesus then guided me to merge my essence with His even deeper. The first thing I noticed was the shift in vibration. He vibrates so highly, it made me, once again, feel lightheaded to be in His Presence. But as I started to merge, I began to feel peace, a quiet strength, and a pervasive feeling that everything, EVERYTHING, was all right.

Stillness, depth of being. What a gift. The intensity was a little overwhelming, and I started to drift away again, but He called me back, challenging me to grow up spiritually. It was not a reprimand exactly, but a strong call to pay attention and get this lesson. The days of flitting around were over. It was time to get serious. Focus, discipline.

I was instructed to merge our minds, and I physically felt an expansion in my head. Then, I was told to merge my heart with His heart. Oh! What a huge, unexpected reaction! My body had convulsions, over and over, for several minutes. Fighting, opening, finally surrendering. Then, it was so amazing. My heart felt bright, clear, big, vibrant! It was the first time I'd ever felt like that.

The next instruction was to link my heart and mind with delicate tendrils of light, but He said they must originate from the heart and join with the mind. In this way, the heart was in control, and the mind would play a supporting role.

He asked me to think about the person I had just been frustrated with. Weird. I couldn't recall the frustration, or the memory of the circumstance. What I saw instead was a person just trying to get through life with her own set of struggles. Oh. I got it. It was surprisingly easy then to surround her with love.

A small, dark, unforgiving thought appeared from my ego, reminding me of what she did. Jesus guided me to send a wave of love from my heart up the tendrils to my mind, my ego. And the dark thought disappeared. Interesting!

I repeated this process with a few others in my "unforgiving" pile. The same thing happened. I felt only love for them. Jesus explained that at His higher vibration, the unforgiving thoughts don't, *can't* exist.

Like vision, we all know that there are many wavelengths beyond the range that we can perceive with our eyes. By raising my vibration to Jesus', through preparation and merging, I could no longer sense or concern myself with those lower thoughts and energies. It's just not possible. With Jesus, there truly is only love.

It was amazing to be in this state of higher vibration, of pure Love. He invited me to return as often as I could. He said that the more I experienced it, the more it would become my vibration too, my way of feeling and experiencing the world. But until that happened, He encouraged me to repeat this experience often.

Responding to my concern about those convulsions at the beginning, He said,

> *The merging of heart energies and all the convulsions opened the floodgates to allow much love energy to flow. When you brought the person you were angry with into your awareness, she was flooded with this love. The convulsions washed away your sins. The flood washed away hers. It is all fresh, new. Be blessed, and be a blessing, sister!*

————

During another session, Jesus said that the day's task was to heal my heart. He asked me to put both hands over my heart and then tell Him what I saw and felt.

Oddly, I saw the heart covered in what looked like grey lichen. It was a brittle, hard shell surrounding my heart. He instructed me to gently clear it away, which I did, carefully breaking off and removing small pieces, one at a time, front and back, to not puncture or damage the heart. Finally, the "lichen" was cleared away, and the heart completely exposed. It was a sickly greyish-pink.

Gently, He infused the heart with waves of life force to reinvigorate it. Only after it took on a healthy glow did He move on to the next step.

Jesus wrote symbols on my heart in that amazing shade of deep green that is His color. The symbols were reminiscent of ones I'd painted. Some of them stayed shining on the surface. Others sank into the depth of my heart. Then He painted the entire heart with a vibrant emerald green, the color of the heart chakra, and the healing was complete.

He told me that I was now to work with Him and learn what it meant, literally, to walk in His footsteps. Archangel Michael, George, and the other angels had prepared me for this and would still be with me, but now I was to turn to Jesus for guidance and instruction.

I'd like to tell you here that that's exactly what I did, but the truth is that I got distracted, forgot, tried to take control, got stressed over job, money, Purpose, you-name-it, over and over again. But any time I needed a chat, He was always right there for me, waiting and happy to connect. Still to this day.

––––

It was Good Friday. I was thinking about what that meant—a reminder that Jesus was crucified and died. It hit me that He did it for us, for me, to show us that death cannot take away the Light because three days later He returned brighter and more vibrant than ever.

That day, in my meditation, He invited me to voluntarily allow an aspect of my ego to die that no longer served me. Fair. Being the over-achiever that I was, I chose two: manipulation and people-pleasing. He told me that those were good choices for me. Those aspects of myself manifested because I had not been ready to stand in my power. That in my perceived smallness, I behaved in this way to get what I wanted. I had different options to work with now.

Thanking Him for this opportunity, I committed to strengthening the positive aspects of power and strength within me, while releasing the old patterns of manipulation and people-pleasing.

Two days later was Easter, and I was remembering why this was a holy day. Closing my eyes, going within, I sent a BIG "Thank you Bro" to Jesus. I shocked myself at those words. They were anything but church-y, but He just smiled. He seemed happy, actually, that we had that good of a relationship, not one all twisted up by religion. There was no focus on holes in hands and feet, or blood running down His face from thorn crown scratches.

He said, *That was a bad moment. No doubt about it. Very bad. But it was in the past. Far past. I've let it go, and you should too.*

I realized how close, and amazing, and loving this man-god was, right in front of me, right within me, heart and being. He continued:

> *Each and every one of you have also had your crucifixion moments. Betrayals, abuses, lost jobs, broken hearts. Moments or circumstances that broke you, killed a part of you inside. Times when you had to bear the unbearable.*
>
> *The next part of my story* (the three days, then resurrection) *can also be your story. Retreat for a time and heal those wounds. Might be three days, might be three or ten years. But CHOOSE to heal.*
>
> *Release, do the very hard work of forgiveness.*
>
> *"Forgive them, Father, for they know not what they do," I said, and felt that deeply, while I was hanging by those nails, knowing I was dying the death of a criminal.*

Yes, if I could find forgiveness in that moment, so can you.

Remember, all that I do, you also can do.

It's not easy, but it's possible.

Then forgive yourself. An even harder task.

Accept and admit you screwed up, or were part of the problem, and extend forgiveness, a clean slate, a start-over, game reset, to yourself.

And then, MOVE ON!

Move on to a new chapter in your life.

Free, wiser, heart and mind healed.

THIS is my message about Easter.

Not chocolate bunnies or Easter egg hunts.

Move on. Find Joy.

Do what you love to do, and let it be, at least in part, for the betterment of others.

You are ALL family. One family. My family. Buddha's family. Moses' family. Mohammed's family. Sun-God and Earth-Mother's family. Tree and rock and whale and bird and ant families.

One big extended family, with all the joys and fights and struggles that exist in any family.

But TOGETHER, we get through.

So calling me "Bro" earlier was not disrespectful. It shows your deep understanding of this "family" concept.

And so I say, "Thank you, little Sis."

BE resurrected, made new, shining in a garment of Light, this day and every day.

Easter is a mindset, a lifestyle, a choice.

Be blessed and know how deeply loved you are.

Wow. I did not see that coming. What a beautiful gift of wisdom and love!

He went on to remind me that He loves us ALL, the hyper, running-around-with-sticky-fingers kids in the family. Getting into trouble, making messes. Like every kid.

Yes, it's like that.
I love you, anyway.
No matter what.
Go ahead. Run around, get dirty, scrape your knees, get tired. And when you're ready, come Home. Home to me. In your heart.
Prodigal sons and daughters.
All of you.
By design.
You don't learn nearly as much by playing life safe.

So, go get lost, get muddy, get your hearts broken, climb amazing mountains. Feel and experience it all. That's WHY you are here!

This life is NOT about playing it safe,
Or playing by someone else's rules.
It's about pushing the edges, kicking up some dust.
It's the only way will you truly discover all the magnificence that resides within you, to activate the hidden knowledge and discover skills and strength you didn't know you had.

So, you see, Easter really isn't about me.
It's about you.
Claim the power of resurrection in your own lives once or thousands of times.

Free yourself from the past and dance into the future. And remember I'm with you, every step of the way.

You are loved. So deeply loved.

What a gift. I was immersed in His energy, so loving and strong that I never wanted to leave. I reread His words several times, feeling them deeply in my heart and throughout my whole body. This was bliss. This was Divine love. Immense, unconditional, freeing. What a joy and tremendous blessing to receive this wisdom from the Master directly—and to call Him friend and brother.

Chapter 17: Reiki Mastery

In the "outer" world, my life was filled with new opportunities to stretch and grow. It was such an exciting time. New experiences and opportunities presented themselves to me easily. For example, a mutual friend told me about someone who was looking for large "spiritual" artwork to hang in his ballroom dance building.

That sounded like fun, another step into *big* art. I arranged to meet him, and we came to an agreement for my first commission. The mural he requested needed to be about fifteen feet long to fit the space allotted for it and painted on canvas, to be framed and hung because the walls were black.

I got a roll of canvas and thumbtacked it to the walls of my art studio. It was so long that I had to wrap it around, using two walls to work on it. Interesting, flowing shapes in shades of pink, peach, yellow, and white, along with a cluster of symbols, filled the canvas.

As I raced to put the finishing touches on it the night before it was to be installed, one section just wouldn't settle, didn't feel right. Just like the office mural earlier. Over and over, I worked on it. Finally, Spirit told me in no uncertain terms to *go home*—that the painting was fine as it was.

Dry by morning, I rolled the canvas up and took it to the dance studio. Patty came and helped build a custom frame for it. I stretched and stapled the canvas onto it, and we hung it on the wall.

The funny part was that I had painted the entire image upside down, and I didn't know it. It was only after it was framed and ready to be hung that I walked around it and realized what I thought was "up" was really "down." The image was indeed perfect as it was.

Mural for dance studio

While I was painting the mural, the owner of the dance studio and I became friends. He even gave me some ballroom dancing lessons. As a child, I loved ballet and thought I would pick up ballroom relatively easily. But it was quite different, and I had two left feet most of the time. Every once in a while, though, it all clicked and then it was magical to glide across the floor in a beautiful flow, somehow embodying the music with synchronized movement.

He had a Karelian camera, which captures a person's aura on Polaroid film. The colors captured correlated to chakra colors: red for root chakra, green for heart chakra, violet for crown chakra, etc.

We had a few fun sessions when he took my aura's image, which mostly showed purples and blues. He told me those colors indicated that I was closely attuned to Spirit. Well, I certainly was trying to be.

Aura photographs of me

We also did an experiment with other people, taking their aura's photo, then asking them to look at one of my paintings, then reshooting their aura. In each instance except one, their aura migrated up the chakras, shifting from orange and yellow to blue, for example, after viewing the paintings. It was informal research that we were doing, for sure, but it suggested that the paintings could have a positive effect on people. Maybe, maybe not, but it encouraged me to keep going.

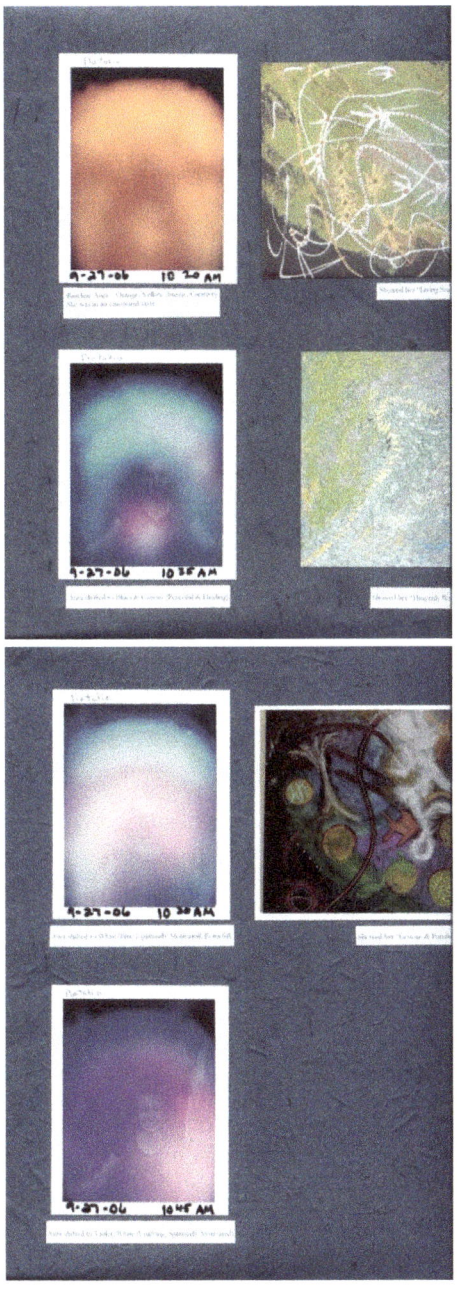

Experiments showing aura shifts after viewing one of my paintings

It turned out the dance studio owner was also a Reiki master. When he found out that I had received two Reiki attunements a while back, he asked me why I hadn't become a Reiki master yet. I told him that I didn't need or want it, that I felt the title of "master" was a bit pompous and off-putting. I had only intended to use Reiki for creating art in the best possible energy.

He told me that the term "master" in Reiki meant "teacher." He also said that I was channeling a great deal of energy, and that if I didn't get the master level attunement, my body would soon suffer. He likened it to running high voltage electricity through wires that weren't strong enough to conduct it and burning out. When he put it that way, I agreed to let him attune me, which expanded the amount of energy my body could process safely.

After my attunement, we did some joint Reiki sessions on a few of his clients. It was an interesting experience. I could feel his energy, very yang—pushing and pulling the energy where he felt it should go, as opposed to the much more yin approach I took of allowing the energy to inform me where *it* wanted to go in the way Patty's teacher had taught me. I liked my way much better.

In the months that followed, I experienced fully the off-handed comment made in the first Reiki class I took. "After you are attuned, anything that no longer serves you in your life will go away." I hadn't connected the dots before with my marriage and home, but I was soon to see that receiving the Master level of Reiki accelerated change in my life even more.

Chapter 18: A Home of My Own

Although Patty and I got along quite well, I eventually became restless living in someone else's home and started looking for a home to buy, even though I did not have a traditional job. Even though my savings account was dwindling. I had complete faith that if the move was appropriate, Spirit would open the way for it to happen effortlessly, and that somehow, the money I would need to live there and pay my bills would be available.

Sure enough, I found a lovely little home on a quiet street, with many large live oak trees providing natural shade and protection from the hot Florida sun. When I found it, it was in the final stages of a remodel—a flipper home. The nice guy doing the work even offered to let me pick out the carpet.

After settlement, but before the new carpet was laid, I took big Sharpie markers and wrote affirmations, inspirational quotes, and symbols all over the concrete floor, setting a foundational energy of peace, prosperity, and well-being for me and anyone else who might come to visit. I found gently used furniture at reasonable prices and hung my paintings on the bare walls, my own personal art gallery—a space to reflect me back to me.

It was a gift of time and space to discover who I had become since those dark days after the downsizing and the divorce. It was a space all my own that enabled the artwork and creative process to expand and pull me forward.

It was the perfect human chrysalis—a retreat, sanctuary, playground, classroom. The time I spent there was blessed. Friends came when invited, and we had wonderful get-togethers. When they left, I regained the solitude I craved.

It truly was a time of self-reflection, of fierce, unrelenting self-focus. It was probably exhausting for my friends, even boring. But it was of the utmost urgency for me. It was a necessary narcissism of seeing all that I had been, clearly and without judgment, and choosing what to discard, carry forward, or transform.

My meditations went deeper and longer than ever before—an hour, maybe two, immersed in that pure love energy. Night after night, I snuggled up to a cozy, comforting fire in the fireplace, fueled with twigs and branches gifted by my trees. (Yes. Florida winter nights can be chilly!)

I had freedom—the freedom to create, or not. To spend time in the yard, getting to know the trees and plants that shared this space with me. To hold art classes, Reiki classes, and energy healing sessions in my home, I gardened and did consulting work as opportunities presented themselves. I began to allow the work to find me, rather than frantically marketing myself. Somehow, I always had just enough money to get through each month.

I stopped fretting about things as much. My ambition and drive faded, and I floated through my days on the raft, finally surrendering to the liquified state of being within the chrysalis—the betweening. Maybe that's a made-up word, but it fits, and I like it.

Chapter 19: Sharing

I knew by then that creating art, at least the way I had been shown to do it, was clearly a powerful path to self-healing. It allowed deeply buried emotions, hurts, and beliefs to surface, without the need to talk about them, and lift them away. Sometimes I felt very uplifted when I painted, and other times I would bawl my eyes out for no discernable reason. Still other times I had to rise above my inner critic to find the strength to simply keep painting and to trust that everything was as it should be.

I found articles, written by professionals in both traditional medicine and alternative healing fields, that acknowledged that art, and other creative endeavors, enhance and complement the healing process, stimulating one's imagination through creative expression encouraged joy, hope, and pleasure. It also was an essential ingredient in confronting, and dealing with, life's obstacles, and opening to new possibilities and solutions.

My perceptions thus confirmed by the experts, I set out to share what I had experienced and learned from others. I loved the idea of combining my two passions, art and healing, into something good.

I volunteered at an organization that helped children process grief through role play, games, and artistic expression. I facilitated art sessions for adults overcoming addictions. While these were interesting and good experiences, I frankly was not sure those folks were ready to heal or were open to art being their healing modality of choice. Still, I offered the best that I had to give at the time and left it up to them to take away whatever resonated.

I created and offered Art for Self-Healing classes, both out of my home and at other venues.

The first class was a "No Mistakes" art class, geared for people who felt that they had no artistic ability. This fear has been embedded in so many people, me included. My seventh-grade art teacher gifted me that, making it clear that, in her opinion, I had no artistic ability at all.

One moment stands tall in my memory. She criticized a drawing I did in class. The composition was all wrong, the people looked like stick people, and it was unimaginative. She humiliated me in front of the whole class. I still remember it in agonizing detail.

Needless to say, I didn't enjoy her class or art in general for a while. And frankly, I still can't draw. Maybe I bought into her judgment, or maybe she was right. About drawing anyway. But it didn't stop me from exploring other types of art.

Then in high school, I tried my hand at pottery and really enjoyed it. I liked the feel of the clay in my hands, and I liked learning how much water was just right for creating shapes that would mold and hold together. I turned a ball of clay into a little Scotty dog, and it turned out okay! I coiled snakes of clay and made a delightful pinch pot, polishing it smooth with a tumbled stone.

My dad built me a kick wheel in the basement, based on instructions we found in a *Popular Mechanics* magazine. I saved up my money and bought a small kiln. I taught myself to throw clay, fire it, and glaze it. It was a fun hobby that ultimately led me to doing demonstrations at a local historical site for tourists.

In eleventh grade, I had a great teacher who encouraged us to enjoy art. I made a scratchboard portrait of a native American man, using the photo on the back cover of an *Arizona Highways* magazine for inspiration. This was the kind, wise Grandfather spirit who came to the party in the grove. It turned out surprisingly well and still hangs over my desk. I always feel loved and protected near him.

High School art project of Native American Grandfather.

When people learned that I was an artist, many would tell me that they couldn't do art, that they didn't have any skills, that they were stuck, like I was in seventh grade, believing someone else's opinion or being intimidated by artists. "Traditional" art can do that. My preference for acrylics, rather than oils, made many a "real" artist look down their nose at me. Oh well.

But I had found something very different and powerful, embedded in the creative *process*. This is what I wanted others to experience. I wanted to teach the art of expressing something that had nothing to do with technical competence of a particular medium or style of art. I knew I could help people learn to listen to their inner guidance through painting, thus releasing those limiting judgments.

I designed the No Mistakes class to be a very non-threatening invitation for people to dip their toes into artistic waters. To discover, maybe accept, that there are no mistakes in creativity, just perfection yet to be realized. To hopefully discover their untapped potential and expand their vision of themselves. As I'd learned, lessons in creative expression are really lessons about how to live, from the heart, in the moment, in the flow.

My flyers invited the curious with the following:

> *In this type of art, there are no mistakes.*
> - *It is about listening, hearing, and paying attention to the small voice inside.*
> - *It is about expressing the feelings that exist in the body, rather than the images that exist in the mind.*
> - *It is about not knowing what you will paint next and loving the surprises that emerge on the paper or canvas, from your hands.*
> - *It is about taking what looks like a mistake and discovering the secret perfection it contains!*

One of my art classes

The classes were well received, with many students asking for a next-level class to continue exploring their creative potential. I took the request into meditation to see what Spirit would suggest regarding topic(s) and approach. What I was given was a huge surprise and magnificent!

The entire workshop, including the topics, structure, and detailed outline, were given to me in a three-hour span, from 4 to 7 am. It filled seven sheets of flip-chart paper. What a fabulous gift.

Much of the information in the workshop was not new. Similar concepts could also be found in other places, such as books, CDs, and movies. However, the power of *this* workshop was that the concepts were introduced, discussed, and *then* integrated into the students' consciousness through the intentional act of artistic creation. During the "download" for the class, I learned that by integrating new thought forms with creative action and intent, life could transform in swift, miraculous ways.

The workshop turned out to be a seven-session series, three hours each, which I named "The Art of Creating Your Best Life." The workshop was very well received, with students telling me afterward that although they had heard or read about the concepts before, they were able to connect them to their own lives at a deeper, more life-changing level.

——

Around the same time, I was also gifted beautiful, uplifting words in a meditation—a free-flowing poem of sorts. I was further encouraged to make a little booklet out of them, which I did, titling it *I See Your Light*. I was even shown how to print the pages so the booklet would come together properly. (This was before the days when software could do that for you!)

I printed a handful of the booklets, hand-bound them, and gave them to my friends. Several asked for more copies to give to *their* friends. I spent a busy few weeks printing and assembling these little booklets, and I even made a little bit of money while I was at it.

Chapter 20: Commissions

Everything was going rather well. My art was being shown in multiple galleries. I was creating beauty on a grand scale, relatively speaking, just as the angels had predicted. I was teaching art classes, offering healing sessions, and connecting regularly with Spirit. Life was interesting, expanding, and dare I say fun? All I needed was steadier income.

I received my first commission to create a painting for a friend. It was both a challenge and a gift. This quickie $150 painting took *many* hours and lots of paint. My mind still had an unfortunate habit of breaking work down to an hourly rate, and my hourly rate was quickly dropping not only below minimum wage, but into the range of coins.

I was seriously challenged to allow the painting to emerge unsullied. Money changed things. Creating was no longer just for joy or Connection. I didn't expect that at all, but if I wanted to support myself in this way, I'd better figure it out.

I was also challenged by Spirit, instructing me to incorporate glitter into this painting. Glitter? *Glitter?!* Glitter is for craft projects! *This is art!* No way! Ego had a nice little hissy fit.

I should have known better. But apparently, I needed to relearn to release resistance, stay open to new possibilities, and follow guidance without an argument, which I did, eventually, more or less, with some grumbling under my breath.

The completed painting turned out to be surprisingly powerful, thanks to the glitter, I must admit. The glitter amped the energy of the painting. I never expected that either. Overall, the painting was unlike anything I had created thus far. It looked almost like a jigsaw puzzle, which is why I named it "Puzzle." The best part was that my client loved it.

Puzzle

Another request for a painting came soon after from the arborist who trimmed my trees. He was *much* more than your typical tree guy. He understood trees at a spiritual level and worked *with* them to optimize their health, while also meeting the owner's needs.

He shared with me that trees live in community, work together to break the winds, and even share nutrients if necessary. He pointed out a very tall tree in my neighbor's yard. "See how it's been trimmed? All the lower branches have been cut off. That will make the tree very unstable in high winds and weaken it in general. Trees actually need branches all along their trunks to gather enough nutrients to feed themselves."

After my trees had been attended to, he asked if I would create a painting for him with trees as the theme. Gladly! Although I'd never painted a tree before, somehow the painting came to life. It even turned out to be a bit whimsical, a description I never thought I'd use for any of my work. There was a large tree in the center with a spiral walkway up its massive trunk for people to climb and live in its canopy. (Maybe the *Star Wars*' Ewoks were my subconscious inspiration.) A gentle river wound its way through the forest, and orbs played in the air.

Standing ones

I was very excited when I received yet *another* commission. This one was from someone who found my art online. I didn't know him. I was on a roll! I started his painting with the best of intentions and worked on it for nearly a year.

In the end, unfortunately, I was unable to let it go. By the time it was completed, it had become much more than a commissioned piece to me. I agonized over this and offered my profuse apologies to him. He said he understood and thankfully held no animosity toward me.

It was a large painting, 54" x 54", requiring a lot of repositioning to comfortably reach all parts of the canvas. I approached the large expanse of blank canvas as I always did—waiting for inspiration, then following the guidance given.

I started by applying modeling paste, swirling and texturizing it as I went. Letting my inner child play, I applied it with no particular plan in mind. It laid the foundation for all that would come, but all I saw then was a frozen sea of textured white on white.

As the modeling paste dried and shrank, cracks formed, and I carefully filled them in. After everything was whole and dry, I began to cover it with a variety of paints, including metallic fabric paint, and, yes, glitter. I even mixed in a variety of essential oils to infuse my intentions, such as Harmony, Peace, and Highest Potential.

I painted in every orientation, both on the wall and flat on my dining room table. The art was a confusing jumble of colors, textures, and patterns. I painted layer upon layer upon layer, using thirty, maybe fifty layers of paint or more in some places. It had *a lot* of layers. Thankfully, some parts of the painting settled in quickly and easily, while other sections remained as restless as the ocean, requiring me to paint over areas that I thought were complete again and again.

The internal guidance that I got for the painting went something like this:

Green, here, please. Now, wash over that with this shade of blue. A little more green now please, but use that *green over there. And let's use the angled brush, okay? Thank you!*

I experienced times of intense creativity when I'd paint at all hours of the day and night until my back sent up a white flag of surrender. I also went through weeks of gestating, waiting for the next wave of inspiration to come.

Directionally, I had no idea where the painting was going nor when it would be finished. But it felt like not any time soon. I worried that the man who commissioned the painting would lose faith in me and not like the outcome. Self-doubt and criticism frequently kept me company, almost convincing me that I had it all wrong and this was just a confusing mess on a very large canvas that was eating up my time and my life.

My mind kept trying to see the finished result, to have an image to strive toward, like the raft's ultimate destination. I was still dog-paddling—even with this painting. But each time I thought I caught a glimpse of something (like the profile of a lady's face), I'd end up painting over it.

This "Teacher" nearly caused me to stop painting altogether. It went on and on and on, with no clue where it, or I, was going. I truly thought I'd either already lost my mind, or that I was about to. Even up to the day of completion, I still couldn't see it.

What was to be my last day working on it, I dug deep once again to find the patience to paint another day. After studying the painting for a while to see what to do next, a small area in the center of the painting called for some basic titanium white paint. Just a smidge. It was completely out of character with the rest of the work—not metallic, not glitter, but flat Ti White. Okay. Shrug. Follow the guidance.

A few quick brushstrokes later, I heard:

Ah, it's done!

"It is?"

Yes!

"Oh... What *is* it?"

Hang it on the wall. No, not that way, turn it around! Now, walk away, turn around, and take a look.

And there it was. An expanding heart. A heart, damaged and crushed, being pulled, maybe ripped, open by an angelic-looking being. On the left side, it looked like a womb filled with new little areas of color. Maybe they represented possibilities of happiness yet to come? And that little section of Ti White? That was where the Light shone through.

Expanding Heart

Yikes! It happened again—just like the mural at the dance studio. The unseen beings who painted this with me knew that they had to *trick* me into creating something my mind couldn't fathom. Paint upside down. Paint in every orientation, wall and table.

> *Let's completely confuse the girl, then surprise her at the end! Sounds like fun, right?*

I could swear I heard some giggling and snorting from the "other side."

Hmph.

In the end, of course, it *was* perfect. All these years later, I am still amazed at the process and that even when I knew the painting was done, I couldn't see what it was. Until they showed me.

It's obvious that this heart was not a gentle lotus flower opening its luminous petals. It was a mess, in the process of being wrenched apart. But that was the point. The blows and wrenching were *necessary* to get the heart to open, to allow the Light to shine through.

And then I understood. Every disappointment, betrayal, and personal failure in my life had closed my heart a little more. It was no wonder that despite my desire to be upbeat, kind, and spiritual, I was far too often still angry, frustrated, and bitter.

Jesus broke into my negative musings and said,

You can die to your anger. Give that willingly to Me. Each time anger, fear, anxiety, or frustration rise up, go into your heart and merge with Mine. You have learned that those emotions cannot exist at My vibration. Expand into it and find peace and balance again.

Reach inside and discover the kinder, gentler Kathy who is buried under all of the emotional muck and help her come out to see the light of day again.

Open yourself to joy and gratitude.

Be a helping angel when you can.

Each moment is an opportunity for a new start.

But you have to get out from under your rock. This whole situation is meant to smoke you out of your den.

I cannot work with you when you are angry and stuck. But I can when you choose joy and gratitude and when you are moving forward.

All will be well.

Each day, remember to stay embodied in the present moment, wherever you are.

Be your own best friend.

Give yourself encouragement and embrace your life, even when things feel scary.

Open your heart, dwell there, and I will dwell there with you.

Expand our shared vibrations out to the world as often as you can.

Seek out joyful, happy experiences.

It's up to you to create your future based on your present thoughts, state of being and vibration. What you put out, you receive back. You know this.

So choose love and joy and gentleness.

Jesus hadn't given up on me, even though *I* had almost given up on me. He helped me see that all the blows to my heart over the years were gifts. And I realized in that moment that my heart had expanded and filled with Light, like the painting, for the first time.

Chapter 21: Hard Lessons

At this point, I had invested several years developing my artistic abilities and portfolio, with little financially to show for it. Friends occasionally purchased a painting. I cobbled my way through with consulting work, healing sessions, and teaching.

As time went by, more and more of my IRA was being used to support myself, to buy time until I had *The Breakthrough*. I knew it was coming. It had to be—the next show, the next class, the next person I met. My antennae were constantly on high alert for an opportunity to present itself that would move me forward as a professional artist and secure my world financially.

Never mind the little voice that reminded me of what I didn't want to hear.

We are going to take you down to zero, to rock bottom, before you can rise again.

I continued to exhibit my art, faithfully attending the openings. I was ever hopeful that a painting would sell at one of the shows, but each time I was disappointed.

I noticed it was not just me though. The people attending the openings were friends and family supporting their artist, just like my friends were doing for me. There were no art collectors among them. Not a lot of commerce was going on for anyone.

I got a consulting job with one of the gallery owners, helping him develop a marketing plan to increase clientele and sales. It was fun and creative in its own right. He really liked the ideas I came up with. In return, he offered me the opportunity to have my own show at his gallery. Here it was! Finally, *The Breakthrough!*

I prepared a proposal for the show. It took me a long time to write my artist statement, to capture the essence of my creative process. I even took a class in crafting a powerful artist statement to make sure it was solid, honest, and truly reflected my work.

I created a theme and a selection of work to be included in the show. I proudly submitted the proposal to the gallery owner, anxious for his glowing feedback and dates for the show. I was a-tingle with excitement! This was My Moment!

What I got instead was not glowing feedback. Instead, he mocked my artist statement, saying, "No true artist writes something like that. Art is a business and all that airie-fairie stuff has no place in my gallery." The show was declined.

I was in shock. I never heard from him again, and I never contacted him. It was not *The Breakthrough* after all.

Between this rejection and lack of sales at other galleries, I stopped exhibiting my work. My heart was no longer in it. It was not worth the trouble or humiliation.

It seemed like exhibiting online could be a more efficient, potentially lucrative way to get my art in front of a global audience. I put quite a few of my paintings on a popular online gallery. I figured I'd let my art speak for itself and the website do the selling.

A month or so later, a couple who saw my art on that website contacted me, wanting to purchase *two* of my paintings! They were willing to pay full price! Ah, salve for my bruised ego. They said they were moving from Opelika, Alabama, to Belgium in the near future, and they asked if they could arrange to have the movers swing by Florida to pick up the paintings for the move overseas. They said they would send me a cashier's check for the full amount plus the cost of the freight. They asked if I would mind forwarding on the difference to the freight company.

When the certified cashier's check arrived, I duly deposited it. Being cautious about getting scammed, I waited a few days to confirm that the check cleared the bank before wiring the shipping portion to the transportation company.

Two days later, I got a call from my bank notifying me that the cashier's check was a fraud. It took a few minutes for that to sink in. Not only was I *not* paid for my paintings, but I was also out nearly $3,000—the amount I wired to the freight company. The bank did nothing to help me recover the money.

I was devastated, scammed after all. And I didn't *have* a lot. My reserves were severely depleted by then. I felt like someone had kicked me in the stomach. I had trouble catching my breath. I felt like vomiting. I cried and cried.

After many *very* bad days, I realized that I had to let it go. In order to move on, to survive this, I had to find a way to forgive the scammers. It took a long while, but eventually I rationalized that they must equate money with love and were so desperate for that love that they would concoct this elaborate scheme to steal it from more trusting souls.

That was the last straw, though. I was done. I was finished with trying to make a living as an artist. Galleries were a bust, both real and online. All my efforts had been in vain. All those years wasted. I was more financially fragile than ever, and I could not have been a bigger failure if I tried.

What was wrong with me? Why couldn't I just suck it up like everyone else and get a job? In truth, I did try quite often, but I was unsuccessful in even landing an interview most of the time. My self-doubt deepened, making it even harder to try again.

———

After beating myself up for living off my retirement funds, I began to view my life from a different perspective. This time and this way of being was a gift and had its purpose. Wherever it was that I was headed, whatever I'd been preparing for, required this dedicated, focused, nontraditional life. The money wasn't mine to horde. The universe, being infinitely abundant, would always provide. My challenge was to gratefully receive the gift of time and space to focus on me and clean every nook and cranny of outdated thinking that held me back.

Every grudge I'd ever held came up for me to look at, release, heal, and finally bless the person I had begrudged. People and situations I hadn't thought of for years resurfaced in my mind. Some were easy to release. Others made me laugh now that I was older. My reason for holding that grudge was just silly. Still other grudges, unforgivenesses, were like wrestling with tigers. My ego refused to let go. But I kept trying.

That Christmas Day, instead of spending money to fly home to be with family, I spent the day alone, surfing job sites and looking for work. After spending hours looking at uninteresting job postings, I found an interesting opportunity to work for an organization that was developing a green think tank nearby. It was similar to Silicon Valley in California, but this one would help new businesses develop alternative energy sources and other environmentally friendly products and services. I wrote to the CEO, was ecstatic to secure an interview, and joined the company shortly afterward.

It was exciting to be on the ground floor of that initiative. It was good to be working and earning money again too! The company had a well thought out, highly complex strategy involving the government, universities, chambers of commerce, and private investors—all working together to support new, economically viable, green businesses. Their visionary, forward thinking was exciting!

When I joined them, the priority was to secure additional funding to get the first phase off the ground. They had one significant investor on board, but they needed several more. I helped them create a presentation that explained the vision and demonstrated the financial benefits of investing.

I also helped them develop two programs for their upcoming Global Green Expo, which was to be held in Orlando later in the year. I developed a Global Heroes program for school-aged kids, patterned after Odyssey of the Mind. Teams of kids would pick a global problem, like an oil shortage or a disruption of the country's electrical grid, research one aspect of the problem, and come up with a potential solution. They were to present their solutions at the expo. I met with several schools and launched the initiative. I also developed an art competition for kids. They were to use recycled materials to create art that would be hung and judged at the expo.

Those were fun projects for me, using both my analytical and creative sides to develop.

We had made a few presentations to potential investors when the CEO received some very bad news. The one key investor backed out, choosing to support a different cause. The CEO was devastated. He had already used up his own resources and was relying on that investor's contribution to cover the organization's short term financial needs, including that week's payroll.

I had just made another withdrawal from my IRA. On a generous whim, I offered it to him, expecting to be repaid the next week. We were clearly full steam ahead, and he needed just a little more time until he had *his* Breakthrough. I knew how that felt. I loaned him a significant amount of money. Five figures.

The following week, the company split in two unexpectedly, overnight. One would focus on developing the think tank, and the other on the Green Expo. Neither side had any cash.

Because of my assignments, I was caught between the two, neither one taking responsibility for my salary. A week later when I showed up for work, the doors were locked.

I realized with horror that I would never see the money I loaned the CEO again, *and* I would not be getting the last three weeks of pay. I sent emails to the owners, which bounced back with invalid addresses. My calls and voicemails were not returned as I tried to pursue what was rightfully mine.

I was furious at being scammed again. People I had trusted, supported, and believed in betrayed me. I was galled that my money had been taken by people claiming to help the planet and do the right thing! I had enough. I was *mad* at them *and* at myself for being too trusting, for letting myself get taken again. I was *really* mad.

My savings, sale from the old house, and consulting work had funded these past years. But there wasn't much left. Spirit apparently had a different perspective. My corporate jobs enabled me to build a very tidy sum in savings. As far as Spirit was concerned, it was there precisely to grant me passage through these past years. There was no secret. There was no betrayal. I was told I'd be taken down to nothing, and it was becoming apparent that it was about to happen. Who knows? Maybe the scamming had purpose too—to help me learn to trust Spirit, and maybe those events occurred to start guiding the raft toward the shore.

Losing so much money in such a short time though, under such devastating, multiple circumstances, was tough to swallow. My body reacted so strongly to the anger raging around inside me that my abdomen turned into a tight, extremely painful ball. I applied Reiki to myself. I said affirmations. No good. Nothing worked.

A friend took pity on me, coming to my home to give me a massage. It was the most excruciating massage I ever endured. I truly thought I was dying. She was able to loosen the knot in my abdomen a little, but then it just spread out over a larger area. I went to bed, applied essential oils, driving them into my body with moist heat, hoping that might help.

However, I knew that real healing required me to accept what had happened. I needed to let it go, as I had in the past. I knew that. Knew it all day. I had tried to come to acceptance, to release my anger in all sorts of ways, but it continued to fester. As I lay in bed, racked with pain and a hot pad on my belly, I asked for help in letting it go.

The first thing that came to me was the three-question mantra, "Can I let it go? Would I let it go? Will I let it go?" Those were simple, but essential questions to answer. In the battle between the ego and the heart who would win?

The ego wanted to be right, to be a victim, to get revenge, justice. It was desperately afraid of running out of money, living on the street, being a failure. Ego intentially blew everything out of proportion to control the situation.

The heart had to take charge to accept, release, and heal what happened. The battle raged on. Every time I made the jump to acceptance, I'd slide back into anger.

Finally, Jesus sneaked in a little suggestion between my racing thoughts. Could I step down the anger to its true components—disappointment and betrayal? When the components combined, the fire burned white hot, but individually their energies would be easier to handle.

Yes, I could step it down. That was much easier to accomplish than to make the quantum leap from rage to release. It's funny that I never thought about that strategy before. I certainly had done more than my fair share of grappling with anger, rage, and betrayal.

Then I got a visual of me as the center of the universe with everything circling around me. Ah, there it was again. I always got in trouble when I slipped into that old pattern, when everything was about me. (*I* was betrayed! What do *I* need?) I ran out of steam, lost my momentum, lost my groove.

That visual was replaced with the universe and me as just a speck, a tiny part of the whole. All things moved together in harmony with no one thing bigger or better than any other. From that vantage point, I could visualize my recent boss. His financial issues *far* outweighed mine, *and* his path was not mine.

In that instant, it became crystal clear that if I hung on to that grievance, I would only hurt myself. That didn't make sense, and it didn't feel good or right. In that one breath, with that one realization, everything shifted. I could effortlessly release the cords of anger and watch them float away like balloons. I could take a deep breath again.

I thanked Jesus for fiercely wrestling me down and whispering that perfect, helpful suggestion in my ear! When I woke up, I was pain-free, at peace, smelling like essential oils, and filled with these words: I am Free. I am Whole. I am Loved. I AM LOVE.

———

On the tail of that experience, I read a powerful teaching by Wayne Dyer, who wrote,

There are no justified resentments. If you carry around resentment, of any kind, towards any person, those resentments will always end up harming you and creating a sense of despair. It's not the snake bite that will kill you. It's the venom. Send blame out of your life. Take responsibility for every choice you have made. Acknowledge that you are here because of those choices. Send love in response to hate, no matter what.

Yes, I learned that the hard way these past few years. It was such a strange time in my life. I was exquisitely happy in my inner world, yet lost and terrified in my outer world—at the same time. Clearly, my time in the chrysalis wasn't quite over yet.

Chapter 22: The Silence

The sudden disbanding of the "Green" organization and the related financial issues it caused me sent me into a tailspin. That had been my first foray back into the working world, and I was surprised to find that I had actually enjoyed the energy and challenges. It also was nice to have my experience in business and strategy development recognized and valued. It made me really sad to lose all that so soon after finding it.

I looked for new, fulfilling directions. My traditional job searches were the same as they had been, extremely disheartening, sending out tens of resumes a day for all types of jobs, from executive level to part-time work at Lowe's. Nothing captured my passion like the tech park had. Eventually, I found a few small businesses that wanted help developing marketing strategies and websites, which I was able to provide. But my heart wasn't into it.

Finally, exhausted, I heeded the small inner voice that kept telling me to just stop everything and focus on discovering a vision for my life. I entered a time of silence, withdrawing from all the busyness of the world, becoming still and listening deeply.

Life somehow rearranged itself, enabling me to experience this sacred time of transformation. I could only trust that I would continue to be supported until this time of silence was over.

It was tempting to continue to keep filling my days with superficial distractions. The Silence insisted that I excuse myself from all this, including watching the news and TV in general and checking Facebook. The Silence challenged me to eliminate all distractions and just *stop*. Just *be* for a little while. I did not know for how long, but knew I couldn't rush or push it. Truly, I could not push the river now. Apparently, I needed to finally experience the wisdom in surrendering to its flow and timing. I simply floated each day on the raft.

It was a process and a spiritual practice. The Silence went against the grain, but slowly, eventually, the stillness began to seep into my Being. In this state of peace, quiet, and calm, I could attune inward more deeply and frequently than ever before.

I found inner wisdom waiting for me, flowing and filling me with new perspectives and inspirations. I wrote, painted, spent time in Nature, took little excursions, and read. I allowed each day to unfold organically in the moment as much as possible, asking what I should focus on and following the suggestions given.

For a month, I spoke with no one. I only left the house to get groceries, fully embracing the stillness within my chrysalis.

During this time, I came face to face with the shame that I had been carrying around, tucked in the dark recesses of my mind. I acknowledged how I treated my colleagues in the corporate days, the inadvertent pain I had inflicted on family and loved ones in my struggle to break free of my old life, and now my inability to financially support myself.

Now the remorse and pain were as though I had inflicted all that hurt upon myself.

Processing shame overwhelmed me and made me physically ill with headache, low energy, lightheadedness, deep despair, and grief. Those old, painful memories resurfaced again and again.

I was suffocating, drowning, and finding it impossible to forgive myself. I was my own ruthless judge and executioner, cutting off all joy and optimism.

I realized that I could not be compassionate or kind to others until I could be that way toward myself. I had to forgive myself, again and again, for my past actions. Forgiving myself was the hardest thing I'd ever done, but life could not move forward until I did.

―――

I came across the story of Dr. Hew Len, which really helped me through this process. Dr. Len was a therapist in the high security ward of the Hawaii State Hospital, where they kept the criminally insane. It was a place of daily brawls between inmates, chronic absenteeism by the staff, and general chaos. Dr. Len applied an ancient Hawaiian healing practice, called ho'oponopono, to treat and heal the patients from his office, without ever seeing or speaking to them.

The essence of ho'oponopono is about taking 100 percent responsibility for everything we see, feel, and experience. I saw it as an extension of the "no justified resentments" that I'd read earlier from Wayne Dyer. Taking total responsibility means that *everything* in our lives is *our* responsibility—simply because it is in our lives.

Literally, from the ho'oponopono point of view, the entire world is our own creation. The circumstances *around* us are merely projections of what is *inside* us, helping us see what *we* need to heal next. The problem isn't with the world, it's with us. For change to happen, we must change our beliefs. And when we change, we change the world around us.

Applying that philosophy, Dr. Len reviewed each patients' files and meditated until he could identify within himself the same behavior or belief that had placed them in the hospital—or at least the potential for having the same behavior. For example, if an inmate was a murderer, Dr. Len asked himself when he had felt like that. Perhaps it was simply to kill a mosquito. The intensity of the crime was different, but the *intent* was the same.

Dr. Len applied ho'oponopono's four simple sentences to himself regarding each transgression. These sentences express remorse, ask for forgiveness, express gratitude, and offer love. "I'm sorry." "Please forgive me." "Thank you." "I love you."

It took Dr. Len four years of this deep forgiveness work, but in the end, it transformed the facility, staff, and patients. Absenteeism fell, the need for medications was reduced, and patients recovered. Ultimately, that part of the facility closed.

———

I found this perspective to be really challenging, but worth exploring, based on the results Dr. Len accomplished. In applying this technique to myself, it was important to really feel into each of the sentences. I needed to truly feel remorse, to humbly ask for forgiveness, to feel the overwhelming gratitude for being forgiven, and to express love to myself.

Taking total responsibility for everything around me, the bad and the good meant no more blaming, no more playing victim, *and* owning everything, even the financial scams and lack of art sales.

Chapter 23: Grace

The book *The Cost of Discipleship* by Dietrich Bonhoffer discusses the concept of Grace, which is God's complete forgiveness of people with a repentant heart. In my struggle to forgive myself, I had forgotten about Grace. But then again, I didn't believe that I deserved it.

But that was the point, wasn't it? None of us *deserves* forgiveness, but God grants it anyway. Humbling.

This reminder made it possible to forgive myself because God had already forgiven me. What was the point of hanging on to my own unforgiveness? Mentally, I got it, but I still struggled to let it go.

I asked Spirit to help me transform the shame into forgiveness.

Spirit's advice was to:

First go from shame to acceptance. Acceptance that past events cannot be changed and that they had purpose, even if I didn't understand it..

I was shown a deck of cards.

The "shameful" moments are like the spades ... just part of the deck. There are also diamonds, hearts, and clubs. Shuffle the deck, expand your awareness to the full breadth of your life, not just on a spade or two.

Same with your financial concerns, or any other aspect of life. You put too much emphasis on that one spade. Best to look at it, then shuffle the deck and put it away. Seek balance, perspective, and Lightness of Being.

With that very helpful visual, I began to develop that bigger perspective.

Chapter 24: Gratitude

During the Silence, I thought back to my corporate days—remembering the power struggles and conflict and wondering what I had done to feed those fires. More ho'oponopono. Taking responsibility for all of it.

Back then, I defined power as 1) control over others, 2) influencing others and/or outcomes, and its sneakier sister 3) manipulating a situation. I was quite adept at all three of those, but after the downsizing, I chose to walk away from all of that, cutting it ruthlessly from my life as I embarked on my spiritual quest. I left "Corporate Kathy" by the side of the road, claiming only "Good Kathy" or at least "Getting Better Kathy" as my persona. Or I tried to.

I was beginning to suspect that my inability to support myself and to grow the art, teaching, or healing businesses was at least in part due to not being in my power anymore. I didn't know how to use power as a spiritually oriented person, in a good way.

I asked Jesus to teach me about power. He said:

Power is creation, creativity, love in action, gained through connection to the universe.

When you tap into this Source by deeply connecting, merging energies, aligning your will, thought, and action to the will of God you realize that Love energy is the driver of all things, all thoughts, all action. Then you are in Power.

Everything is possible in this state. Using your personal power to heal and help people is the best thing you can do.

Stay in the present moment, paying attention to the opportunities offered in each moment. This will move you most quickly along your path. Seek to embody gratitude, openness, flexibility, tolerance, compassion, love.

Recognize God looking back at you through the eyes of others, honoring their divinity and the challenges they have on THEIR journey.

Take time to reinforce your connection to Source, repair any tears in that connection. Like any network, preventative maintenance must be done to keep it clear and strong. This connection is your source of strength and power. That is why taking time to be still and to connect is so important.

Awesome wisdom. Truly. For me, I had to start with directing that love energy first toward me, especially the most unlovable despicable parts of me. Unconditionally. Then I needed to *reintegrate* Corporate Kathy back into my life. I needed her drive, chutzpah, and power to move me forward, but I had to integrate her differently.

Taking Jesus' advice to heart, I started to look for opportunities to help or heal, whether mundane or significant, and approach all of it as though I was doing it for Him.

By observing the world around me more closely, I began to notice how many miracles surrounded me each day, such as a perfect parking spot, a meeting that went well, a great deal at the store, or a perfect solution to a problem. I noticed the trees as I waited at a stoplight. I watched the clouds drift by and morph themselves. I listened to the frogs, crickets, and birds all around me. And I said thank you.

Observing all that was going right in my world, all that was beautiful, had a magic of its own that attracted even more positivity. I could feel Jesus smiling each time I remembered to notice and give thanks.

———

For me, "receiving" had always been difficult. So often, when offered help, I'd automatically say, "No, that's all right. I've got it." It took me a long time to understand that in that moment, I had just turned away a beautiful gift.

A lifetime of being disappointed or let down by others taught me to become fiercely independent, relying on myself to get things done. My ability to receive help, receive Grace, receive *anything* atrophied. And maybe, if I'm honest, some of the things I did in the past made me feel unworthy of receiving good things.

Patiently, Jesus showed me a better mindset that permitted receiving, and why.

> *Allow the Love of the Creator to come closer. Receive it.*
>
> *Allow it to transform from a conceptual Unconditional Love to a personal acceptance of "I Simply Adore You!" from the Creator.*
>
> *Move the Love from your conceptual mind to your heart.*
>
> *Can you do this?*
>
> *Can you receive and accept the words "I Adore You" from the Divine into every cell of your Being?*
>
> *Can you say them to yourself, about yourself?*
>
> *You will know when you have learned to truly Receive when you can step fully into the energy of that Adoration and then reflect it back and outward.*
>
> *Balance in all things is desirable.*
>
> *To receive allows another the blessing to give.*

To receive acknowledges the blessing of the gift given.
Receiving can be as simple as stopping in wonder at a sunrise,
or accepting a helping hand.
You cannot give what you have not first received.

Once again, I was humbled and overwhelmed with Jesus' simple yet profound wisdom. He made receiving sound like a good thing! Like the others, that lesson would take years to integrate.

As if in confirmation of all this, while I was working in the yard I heard:

Until you know how loved you are, you cannot move forward.

When I looked up, I saw a beautiful spiderweb and spider. The pattern on its belly looked like a happy face. Message received!

I was finally becoming friends with a vaguer notion of destination. I was continually amazed at how Love could truly make anything happen, such as emails from friends filled with gentle humor, deep love, and messages of encouragement. I received them with an open and grateful heart.

Sitting in front of a fire in my fireplace, I remembered the magnificence of Florida sunsets, and comradery of friends. One memory led to another, and another, all reminding me of how loved and cared for I was.

As I watched the final embers glow, I offered a pinch of tobacco in gratitude and reverence to all those who had assisted me on my journey. I was so happy and full of joy, love, peace—all the good stuff. My heart could not contain it all, and my eyes filled from the potency of the emotion.

Chapter 25: The Chrysalis Splits

One day, I was on my way to a friend's place to give her a healing session. On the way, I saw a recently hit red-tailed hawk in the middle of a busy four-lane highway. Seemingly of its own accord, my car turned into a nearby parking lot.

As I parked, I realized that I was supposed to pick up the bird and take it with me. Although the red-tailed hawk was my primary power animal at the time, it was also a protected species. Still, it was already dead, and my team was telling me in no uncertain terms to get it off the street.

How? I didn't have a bag or a towel or a blanket to pick it up with.

Look for a bag along the side of the road. There's always trash there.

Sadly enough, there *was* a plastic grocery bag. I picked it up, scooted out to the bird between cars, placed it inside the bag, and carefully placed it in the trunk of my car.

Prior to that moment, I would have been ecstatic to find just one hawk feather, which I always took as a message of confirmation, love, and support. But to have a sacred bird, *my* sacred bird, in its entirety was an over-whelming blessing. I sent deep gratitude to Spirit and to my power animal for gifting this messenger to me.

I continued on to my friend's place, performed the energy session, and headed home. It was clear that I needed to do something with the bird. But what? It couldn't stay in the trunk of my car. Not surprising, when I got home, each step was revealed to me, just when I needed to know it. Just like painting, or healing.

First, I lit some sage, blessed the bird and myself, and thanked it for its life. I felt all the way down into my bones that this unexpected gift was a sign that my new life was about to begin.

When the hawk struck the pavement, one shoulder was broken and smashed. The rest was in excellent condition. I retrieved a pair of pruning shears, as instructed, picked up the bird and headed to the backyard.

As the sunset painted the sky overhead in majestic oranges and reds, I cut away the hawk's wings, the good shoulder, tail, and feet with gentle care and reverence. I plucked the remaining feathers from the body.

I laid the remaining carcass in the very back of the yard for nature to reclaim, again as instructed. Taking the harvested parts into the garage, I made a slurry of the remaining sage embers, Epsom salt, and water. Gently, I rinsed everything in this mixture, then rinsed again in just salt water. With the wings slightly folded, I laid out all the pieces on paper towels to dry.

The next morning, I opened and slowly preened each feather so it would dry into its natural shape, taking several minutes each to reform its shape. It felt like a holy task.

The wings were so beautiful, delicate, and strong. They created a gentle breeze when fluttered. *The Breath of Life,* I heard,

We are all One; we all breathe the same Breath.

One wing bone had broken in the fall, reminding me how fragile life is. The tail was opened for balance at time of impact, reminding me to stay balanced during life's unexpected twists and turns. The feet, dried with talons extended, were symbols for grasping, and holding, the right opportunities when they came along.

It took some time for the stink of death to leave the garage. I found a nice box to store the hawk in, with sage sprinkled throughout, and white silk scarves gently wrapped around each piece. I sorted the loose feathers into separate boxes to be used at some unknown time in the future. I was in awe of this gift from my power animal, a physical reminder of our special connection.

———

Shortly after, I had an integrative healing session. The therapist had a remarkable way of listening to the body and energetically providing what it needed in a gentle, soothing way. I looked forward to this session with her because I knew I'd come away feeling peaceful, balanced, and put back together.

The session was beyond my expectations. She homed in on my left thigh and said there was what seemed like a worm coming out of an apple, indicating that a trauma lodged there was ready to be released.

She gently touched my thigh, here, pause, and there, pause. I felt a blazing light run through me, healing and sealing the wounds. Tendrils of light infiltrated my body in delicate wisps, working their way slowly, relentlessly, gently from my crown throughout my body. Every cell inhaled this new infusion of light. I felt a huge shift in my crown and heart, like I was being roto-rootered, cleansed, brightened from the inside out.

I search for better words to describe this feeling, but none suffffice. It was a "beyond words" experience, similar to what I had occasionally felt in deep meditation, but that day it was far more intense.

When we were done, she recommended that I go straight home and sleep to integrate the changes, which I did, sleeping straight through till morning.

This beautiful new energy was now fused and crystallized within me. I felt solid, grounded, expanded as never before. My heart felt so alive, like a ball of energy.

––––––

The next day, a friend came over to trade energy work. We took turns working on each other. She studied different modalities than I, preferring Donna Eden's approach to balancing energies.

I got up on the massage table I had in my "healing" room.

Soon after the session started, a powerful thunderstorm kicked up out of the blue, as sometimes happens in Florida. The wind thrashed the house, and the rain came down in heavy sheets. Even though it was midafternoon, the sky darkened like dusk.

A bolt of lightning cracked right by the house. I watched as it hit the ceiling fan right above me, sending a bright ribbon of energy down and striking me. It felt like a fist had hit me in the chest, up and to the right of my heart, knocking the wind out of me. Then it moved, instantaneously, through my chest, up my neck and out my ears. It was the strangest sensation. Fortunately, except for that initial punch, I was unharmed.

In the aftermath everything stopped for a minute while we gathered ourselves. What had just happened? Was I okay? Was she okay? Was the house ok? She said she felt the energy come into the room but that it missed her.

The upper right part of my chest felt sore and a little swollen. (To this day, I can still feel where the lightning "kissed" me.) My friend found my assemblage point (where the soul connects to the body) blown away from my body about eight inches. In my mind's eye, I could see it as a high voltage wire, just hanging there, shooting sparks.

She felt it was there for a good reason, that the lightning had blown away something that was no longer needed. She strengthened my heart and built a bridge for the soul to reconnect with my body when it was ready. I was not aware of this technique or assemblage points, but I was very grateful that she was with me when it happened and could perform this sort of energetic triage.

The entire house lost power. I assumed the whole neighborhood was also out, but I couldn't tell because it was still light outside. I manually opened the garage door, and we went out for dinner. It seemed an odd thing to do in that moment, so mundane, but we both needed a little time to process that remarkable experience.

When I got back, it was getting dark out. The power was still out at my place, but all my neighbors' houses were fine. I called the power company, who sent someone out to check. While I waited for him to come, I picked up sticks in the yard. I discovered two railroad ties, which had been just outside the healing room, edging a little garden, blown in half and hurled almost into the neighbor's yard. Yikes. Was I lucky!

Turned out the house had a blown breaker. The garage door opener was fried, as was the washing machine, but thank God everything else was fine: computer, A/C, refrigerator, and even the ceiling fan that took the hit.

What a miracle! I was grateful that everything was okay, or at least repairable, and that I was fine. I wondered why the lightning came inside my home and hit me. It was no coincidence, of that I felt sure.

My friend joked that I had received an attunement directly from God. I don't know. Maybe she was right. Two huge energy shifts in a row—the day before at the healer's and now with the lightning was odd indeed.

Two days later, I was restless and had trouble settling down. Maybe it was a result of the lightning strike, but I didn't have any ambition at all. My brain told me I should be out looking for a job, but I just couldn't get focused or motivated.

What was wrong with me? I was getting dangerously close to the "down to nothing" state, but I didn't care. Or maybe, at a subconscious level, I sensed that my circumstances were beginning to change.

There must have been some purpose for everything that had happened, and I had finally stopped fighting it. If I was meant to ramble around the house, removed from the daily grind, then so be it. I had given up control of my life and was floating down the river on the raft.

I was unconditionally loving myself and disassociating from my critical thoughts, reaffirming that I was loved, safe, and exactly where I should be at that time.

I was so confused about my life though. When measured against society's rules, it was a terrible mess, but there must be new rules in place, right? This was a new world, and I didn't know how it worked yet. I wished I understood my apathy and what I should do, or not do, or think, or not think.

Seeking answers, I turned to the digital I Ching on the computer. I know, funny, right? I had much better sources for guidance at hand. But I checked it anyway. Interestingly, the message it gave me was spot on when it told me that men have gone mad waiting for the fates to release them. I felt like I had gone mad too.

Yet I had a tenacity to keep holding on one more day, and one more day, like when I painted *Expanding Heart*. With every attempt I'd made to break the cycle or do something with art, healing, or teaching, I'd been slammed right back down again.

I was out of patience and out of my mind with restlessness, stress, and anxiety. Was it better to wait for Spirit to release me or should I look for a job?

It would have been so easy to beat myself up as a failure, an idiot. I'd done that a million times. Instead, this time I chose to focus on unconditionally loving myself. I chose to stand *with* myself through this crazy time. Or at least I tried to.

Honestly, I did feel like a failure at times. Well, maybe not so much a failure but the butt of a big joke. I could not be faulted for my intent or effort. I wanted so badly to be out there, using my mind and talents for good—in Service. I wanted to be a mentor, manager, or something *useful*. I felt so useless knocking around the house, clueless, waiting, waiting ... for what?

I could not get excited about any job I'd looked at. And the ones I could get a *little* excited about slipped away from me.

Some days it seemed impossible to pull out of my feelings of despair and hopelessness. Why had I been given these gifts and then made to watch them stall out every time I tried to use them? My life was completely crumbling around me. I had no money, no job, not even any signups for my classes.

What scared me the most was my lack of caring about anything anymore. I felt so beaten down, defeated, and confused. What was I doing wrong? What did I need to do to get my life back on track?

I knew I was supposed to be practicing loving myself unconditionally, and actually I might've been doing a little bit better at it. I should have been jumping out of this malaise and helping others—a tactic that usually got me back on track—but I didn't even care or want to bother. What was the use? I was stuck, and I saw no way out.

I was getting myself mentally prepared to lose the house. What would I do with all the paintings? Put them in storage for years like the concrete sculpture? I just didn't have the energy to deal with any of it. It took me three days to call to get my washer and garage door fixed.

I was continually on the verge of sobbing, but the tears wouldn't come. I knew that a big storm was brewing, but I could find no relief. How could anyone be so sad?

The next morning, I went to my friend Judith's house to help her with a few things, but she ended up helping me integrate the lightning energy, to welcome it into my body and soul. During the session I heard, *All things are possible.* The sobbing began and it took hours to finish processing and feel more like myself.

The next day, one of my art students came over for a private lesson. What a gift. She gave me an angel magnet and a whale card telling me that I was her hero. It touched me. She told me over and over how my art class started a whole sequence of events in her life that helped her open and heal. She truly had become a different person from the student I met a few months ago.

We painted and talked. As I listened to her, I heard echoes of myself—a people-pleaser who became devastated when she let someone down. I realized that had been my challenge recently too. I felt like I'd let Spirit down, as well as myself because I had focused on my spiritual path—rather than generating income and becoming self-sufficient again.

My student also brought a deck of Sonia Choquette's cards. I pulled the "Self-Control" card. That was a clear message to cease the emotional outbursts and become calm, cool, and collected.

Chapter 26: Final Lessons

One day I realized that I had never actually specified *how* I wanted to serve God. I don't think it ever occurred to me that I had the option to choose. Maybe I did. Maybe I didn't.

Did I ask to be an artist? A healer? No. But once guided onto those paths, I gave it my all to become as accomplished as I could.

Finally, I realized that if I wanted to be a Servant, I needed to finally, deeply, completely learn to trust. I needed to trust that Spirit had the big picture and knew how the pieces fit together when things needed to happen. I knew all this *intellectually,* but the rest of me needed to be on board too. Maybe all this waiting, things not working out the way I thought they would, was getting me ready, teaching me to trust.

But just as importantly, I also needed to become trustworthy. Worthy of Trust. Was I obedient, really? Could Spirit trust *me* to follow Guidance without debate? Would I align my will with Divine Will and release control? Would I hold my balance amid financial crises and lack of clarity? Would I habitually start to move beyond myself to think of others? Or would I get lost in my fears and dramas again?

This was challenging work, requiring lots of repetition and reinforcement. My biggest lesson was that to become trustworthy, I needed an enormous amount of patience.

Spirit's timing is Spirit's timing. Period. Patience had never been my strong suit, but getting frustrated, anxious, rebellious, and demanding did nothing but delay things.

I also wondered if wanting to be of Service wasn't similar to someone who wanted to be a Marine. They had to get through boot camp first. Maybe these past years were my bootcamp.

I know a little about boot camp. Years back, after my son's freshman year at college, he came home and announced that he was going to join the Marine Reserves, spending the summer in boot camp in North Carolina. Boot camp? What happened to me spoiling him all summer, lounging at our pool, soaking up the sun, and going shopping?

Nope. My son knew his path and he ran down it fearlessly. He would not settle for anything less than the Marines. They were the elite, the toughest, the ones to be there when all hell broke loose. And he wanted to be part of it.

Cellphones were not allowed at boot camp, so I had no direct communication with my son. At the end of the summer, I drove to Parris Island to attend his graduation. I hate to admit it, I did not recognize him. I literally looked right past him in my eager search for his face, his profile.

He was skinny! Last time I'd seen him, after coming home from college, he was bulked and muscled from months of college food and hours at the gym. Mr. Body Builder, meet Mr. Lean and Mean.

And he wore "BC" glasses, instead of contacts. BC stood for "birth control," meaning the glasses were so ugly that no one would want to kiss him.

But the thing that was most changed about him was his energy, his essence. No more cocky kid with an attitude. This was a Marine in front of me—disciplined, focused, polite. *Polite?* What *did* they do with my son?

What I learned about boot camp from him was that it's a process, required for entrance into service, and you come out different, stronger, prepared.

What I learned that day, and what I continue to understand, is that the transformation is complete. It must be. The old identity, values, and weaknesses must be stripped away before the newer, stronger persona can emerge. Resistance, stubbornness, and tenacity eventually, inevitably, give way to acceptance, fluidity, and grace. It's a different kind of chrysalis.

More than anything, I wanted to be on Jesus' elite Team, like my son wanted to be a Marine. I hungered to be of Service, to be an Ambassador of the Divine, to live a life that had meaning—the very antithesis of corporate profit-driven America.

But to do that, I had to go through intense training and preparation, like a Marine. However, I didn't know that when I "signed" up. I didn't know that like the Marines I would be taken down to the last of my strength, endurance, and finances. I didn't know my old life would be stripped and ripped away so that I could be remolded. Rebuilt. Transformed.

What a gift of loving synchronicity that I was reading *Initiation in the Great Pyramid* by Elisabeth Haich at that time. The book is a fascinating memoir of a past lifetime as an initiate in the Egyptian priesthood. She wrote,

The ... initiate has become master of himself. He has been taught to purify and subdue his sensual nature, then to purify and develop his mental nature and finally by utter surrender of his old way of life and losing his soul to save it, he has unfolded spiritual faculties.

The soul must voluntarily and consciously pass through a state of utter helplessness, from which no earthly hand could offer aid or rescue. He must walk the Way of the Cross alone, until at length, through initiation, divine help itself descends from higher realms and raises the regenerated soul to union with itself ... raising the incarnated soul to a state of rebirth, regeneration and at-one-ment. Initiation, then, is a symbolic death and a resurrection.

The words clearly explained what had been happening to me. All these years had surely been an initiation just as rigorous as boot camp, as the ancient mystery schools. Life itself was the purifying fire, preparing me for my sacred work.

Every challenging situation I experienced was like solving a math problem or taking a spelling test, helping me learn to make appropriate choices in thought and behavior, to develop mastery over the key attributes of compassion, tolerance, love, patience, and surrender.

Service had been my ultimate ambition, requiring me to move beyond the goals and drama of personal ambition, agenda, and ego. It took me a long time to realize that none of the ideas I had dreamed up for my "purpose" would amount to anything.

I had finally learned that Service would take many forms and change from day to day, moment to moment. Being an Instrument required being tuned in to Guidance 24/7 and understanding that "assignments" would often be different than I expected. The new rules of the road were suspending expectation, embracing a go with the flow attitude, staying sharp, listening to, and acting on, guidance, without question or argument.

The term "Service" might sound like a special title. I now knew it wasn't. It simply meant that I had learned enough along the way to be somewhat helpful to Spirit from time to time.

Spirit truly provided all I needed through unexpected gifts and opportunities reminding me that I had not been abandoned and that all was truly in order and on schedule. My job was to do whatever was presented for me to do each day with a happy, willing, relaxed heart.

I was staying steady, regardless of what life might look like from the outside, regardless of family pressure to get a "real" job and become responsible again. How could my family possibly understand this transformative, alchemical process when I hardly understood it myself?

The next week, a string of synchronicities was simply mind blowing. It was like there truly was magic all around me—even down to getting a new bra from my friend Kay, who was quite differently sized than I. She had found a bra in the back of her dresser that clearly didn't fit her but was perfectly sized for me in a lovely, soft mint color. Only the day before I had been leafing through the latest Victoria's Secret catalog, earmarking a page of bras, and wondering how I could get a new one. Handled and delivered beautifully.

A few months back, I had replaced cable TV for satellite as a cost-cutting measure. But now, as finances continued to dwindle, I wanted to cancel even the satellite service. I could read for entertainment or browse on the computer. But the satellite service was an ironclad two-year contract. They wouldn't budge on ending it early, unless I wanted to pay the entire two years of fees all at once.

One evening, I tried to watch TV, but the satellite service was not working right. Some channels came through okay, but others were completely scrambled. Their remote tech support said that two separate satellites provided the channels and that one of the satellites was not transmitting successfully to my dish, for reasons unknown. He promised they would send someone out the next day.

It turned out that the trees at the back of the yard were blocking the signal from the one satellite. It had been winter when the dish was installed, and the tree branches were bare of leaves so the signal came through, no problem. Now, it was spring, and there was a full canopy of green back there, which blocked the signal. There was no way to remedy the situation.

The satellite TV contract was broken, with no penalty. I was so grateful. Watching Spirit in action, helping me trim my expenses was humbling, awesome, fun, and exciting.

Moments like that buoyed me and allowed me to move forward with utter confidence, rock solid, knowing that all was well, even though I was approaching what looked and felt like utter financial ruin.

I was training, like a Marine in boot camp, to hone the attributes of Light. Training, like an expert tracker, to notice the subtle signs of grace all around me, to observe and experience the magic of the world with heightened senses. I was learning to turn away from mass consciousness, find the courage to be vulnerable, look like a fool and not even notice after a while. Beginning to sustain a state of "present moment," with awareness and focus for longer. Maintaining inner balance with gratitude a little more frequently.

Of course, I slipped back, time and again, but my recovery was faster, and the drop into despair was not as deep and all-consuming.

My friend Kay often observed that I was obedient. I never cared for that term. An old feistiness surfaced every time she said it. I didn't *want* to be obedient. It reminded me of childhood, when I had to suppress my enthusiasm, curiosity, and personality to obey an authority figure— parent, grandparent, teacher, and later boss.

But then I realized that what Kay was really saying was that I was doing my best to listen for, and follow, guidance from Spirit. It was actually a compliment, and it was what I'd been saying I wanted most dearly, to be used by the Divine, to be a servant.

Then Kay's words lifted me up, giving me the morale boost she had intended all along.

———

One morning, I woke with wobbly knees again—acutely aware that money was tight and I had no clear direction. Yet again, I questioned myself about not looking for traditional work, but my gut turned queasy every time I thought about it. I knew there was something coming. I was surrounded and supported every day. What more could I ask? My job was to stay positive and ready.

My shamanic name, Butterfly on Rose, came back to me as I sat out back, noticing several butterflies flitting through my garden. According to *Animal Speak* by Ted Andrews, butterfly is about transformation and shapeshifting. It is also the symbol of the Soul, of change, color, and joy. Butterflies dance, taking life lightly. Dance brings back the sweetness of life. And hasn't that been my journey? To learn to take life lightly? To float on Spirit's gentle wind and know that everything is always as it should be?

I knew I had more layers to shed, more light to let in, and more fears to face and conquer. Yet I felt ready to open my life again. I simply awaited upon Spirit to release me from this chrysalis.

Each day, I asked for guidance, what to do and who to help. One day I was told,

Know that all is well at this moment. Walk in grace, breathe by grace, all that you are is a gift to polish and shine so that you may give it on to others.

I released yet again my need to achieve, to be in control. I had offered my Soul this life—to experience what it wished and to accomplish what I had denied it in past incarnations, due to my fears, limitations, and distractions. It had not been an easy journey thus far. Then I heard the quiet inner voice remind me that few people would take this path, would choose to turn over their lives like I had because the cost was high.

As my financial resources dwindled from once very healthy to now meager, I came to realize that *abundance* is so much more than a big bank account. By then I had experienced a wealth of wrong turns, an abundant supply of brick walls and frustration, and endless depths of unhelpful self-talk.

My inner voice spoke again, encouraging me to open the book *Love Without End: Jesus Speaks* by Glenda Green. Opening it to a random page I read,

When we seek abundance just for ourselves, that's when we get into trouble.

We have to seek abundance for all."

The path to prosperity has been a sacred, powerful journey, taking me inward, revealing outdated thought patterns and uncovering all the ways I limit my experience and expression in this life. My most important wealth can only be found within me.

It led me inevitably to accept myself exactly as I am. Light and shadow, courageous and cowardly. Inevitably embracing my humanity ... and my divinity.

Accepting, loving, cherishing, and honoring myself opened many paths to me, including the path where prosperity and abundance of all good things raced to greet me with open arms.

I had been shown the nature of true abundance, which was so much different than I ever imagined. Now it was up to me to release my old, outdated mental constructs and integrate this new understanding into my life.

Chapter 27: Flight

I had watched the universe arrange for my life to spiral in and quiet down. Grow still. As patiently as I could, I waited for Spirit to choose the time and method for me to break free and fly, transformed.

I restrained myself, foregoing the long-ingrained habits of doing, checking things off a list. I'd lived off my future retirement, watching it deplete. Staying the course felt like folly, looked like lunacy, yet followed a hidden wisdom. It forged and tested trust, inner strength, and courage, again and again. It alchemized ego and pride into readiness, gratitude, and humility.

Shutting down a life so completely could only have been the handiwork of the Maker. Rather than chafing at the bonds and restrictions, I had been asked to relax into the chrysalis and allow myself to be liquified, shaped, and enhanced by the Creator.

But one fall day, I just couldn't settle. A restlessness in me was at cross currents to my planned quiet day. Finally, I gave in to the fabulous weather and raked leaves. I mean, *really* raked leaves. I got them out from under all the hedges that lined the backyard, at times crawling under and between them to get every tiny brown oak leaf.

I disturbed some bees that had a little nest in the hedge. Being allergic to bee stings, this situation could have been very bad. Instead, I stopped, slowed my breathing way down, and sent them love and calming feelings. Very slowly, I backed out, freeing myself from the bush without one sting.

It reminded me of a time when I was a kid in Brownie day camp. I was running down a wooded path, with my mouth wide open, yelling, when a yellowjacket flew right into my mouth. That time too, I stopped running (and yelling) immediately, bringing myself to as much stillness as I could.

The wasp was curious, though, taking a leisurely stroll all around my teeth and cheeks, across my tongue and over the roof of my mouth. Its antennae waved and probed like a blind man with a white cane. It tickled, but I didn't dare laugh. I was terrified that it would sting me or try to crawl down my throat. I hardly dared to swallow.

People started gathering around me to find out why I was just standing there with my mouth open. I couldn't tell them. After what felt like a year, the wasp's curiosity was finally satisfied, and it flew out of my mouth and away.

Maybe that experience helped me deal with the current bunch of annoyed bees.

A trail of bags, full of leaves and branches, stretched from the garage all the way to the street. It cleared a lot of stagnant energy in the yard, and in me as well.

The next day, I went out back to pull weeds, check on the flowers and veggies, and connect with this peaceful space. What I didn't expect was the strong sense that the garden was somehow telling me that it was time to leave. I needed to release the garden, the house, the area. My work here was done. It was time to move on.

Where? How? When? My mind whirled with questions, with an undertone of HELL NO! I had gotten used to my reclusive way of life. I had just gotten the yard tamed from years of overgrowth, and the garden was just starting to produce well. It was just a matter of time until the art, healing, or teaching took off. I just had to hang on a little bit longer.

No, dear. It's time to move on. You have made it to the far shore. Start getting ready. Time grows short.

Those words were a blessing so immense that it took time to actually sink in—to know that this long journey was finally over, and my true work, soul work, was about to begin. For so long, it had been a distant hope, a glimmer, a thread so fine it seemed lost at times.

And now it was here. In a moment, life changed. I had a lot to do to tie up loose ends—organize the office, closets, books, paintings, and garage, file taxes, and tend the garden. The winds of change were upon me.

This place, this sanctuary, had been my chrysalis, completely supporting me for the past year and a half. But now as I began to think about the future, I knew I had to move on. I had no idea where I'd end up, but I trusted that the winds would take me where I needed to go.

My mind began to consider new options. Should I go through personal bankruptcy to eliminate my accumulated debt? No, it did not feel right to abandon my obligations. The house and the car could be released back to the bank and dealership. I felt responsible to repay the credit card debt. I chose to make those charges, and it was my responsibility to pay them off. Another manifestation of ho'oponopono—take responsibility for everything in my life, including my credit card balance.

If I could sell a few paintings, I could clear that debt and start fresh. That would also solve the dilemma of what to do with my art when I moved out. And for real I needed to get a job. The perfect job hadn't dropped in my lap, despite my efforts to find one. I was finally willing to contemplate any job. Better than nothing.

In support of my new-found energy and direction, I received this message:

Lighten the load. Know that this is in highest good. Free up your energy for the road ahead. Do this in joy and grace.

———

Re-entering the world was not an easy task. I job hunted online. I tried to return the car and do the right thing and talk with them before there was a payment issue, but they were holding me to the lease payment, like the satellite company. I was not angry, just confused. I told them that there was going to be a shortfall, but they chose to wait to address it after it became a big problem.

That reminded me of what I'd been doing with my whole financial situation. Well, what was done was done. I could only focus on moving forward with as much grace and courage as possible.

Somehow this would all unfold, not by my brilliance, but by the will and grace of the Divine. And as I'd learned so well, that usually meant at the final moment and in unexpected ways. So be it. I called the mortgage company too, and they also chose to wait.

My friends and family were so supportive of me, which had been such a beautiful gift. Some offered financial support, others a place to land. I felt blessed to have such loving friends and family around me.

With a big sigh, I surrendered to the flow. I released the house and yard with great love and gratitude. I swallowed my pride and called my son, who invited me to come live with him and his fiancée. I hated to move in with them because they were just about to be married, but I hoped it would be a very temporary stop-over on my way to something else.

Events were set in motion, and the logjam that had been my life started breaking up.

I was grateful for Spirit moving me forward, and I asked:

> *Please deliver me safely to my next destination.*
> *Help me navigate the details of this transition.*
> *Guide me toward work that will restore my financial health and help others.*
> *Help me find good homes for the things I no longer need.*
> *Let me feel you walking with me and opening the way for me.*
> *I know deep in my heart that all this has already been handled, but my knees are wobbly, and I could use your loving presence to comfort me and steady me now.*
> *Thank you.*

The move began to take shape. Storage and a moving truck were lined up. I had preliminary conversations with a Realtor to list the house. I hoped for a buyer to take ownership quickly. The place had been so loved, and it had shared its love so freely with me in return.

The chrysalis that had been my home, supporting and protecting me, was no longer needed. My new butterfly self was almost strong enough to fly. My beautiful wings would soon lift me away to destinations unknown. My proboscis was ready to sip the sweet nectar of life.

Conclusion

The precision and beauty of the miracles that came when I chose to walk with Spirit were incredible. Spirit's ability to bring life down to a still point, to strip away everything, to orchestrate catastrophic failure of every source of security and identity was not done to punish, although it felt like that many times, but to strengthen, refine, and prepare me for the next stage of my journey. It was all done with infinite wisdom and love—far beyond my human capacity to grasp, but I accepted it as truth, nonetheless. Why minimize such dazzling grace just because it exceeded my understanding?

In accepting that everything was always well in the universe, I was also coming to accept that all was always well with me too. Self-loathing and contempt, guilt, and shame slowly gave way to grudging acceptance, then to a tentative ability to truly love and honor all parts of me— good, bad, ugly, broken, and magnificent. Finally, I was recognizing the incredible gift of my existence and my gifts with gratitude and humility.

By owning the perfection, the spark of God, that is me, I could acknowledge the same in others. I could honor and celebrate the beauty and perfection of their journey, to bear witness to it, lend strength when needed, yet know it was theirs alone to travel, at their own pace, in their own way. I emerged from the chrysalis a more loving and supportive observer, rather than a meddling fixer of other people's lives.

Spirit guided, enabled, and fine-tuned my transformation and announced my rebirth. But it was up to me to break free, to take the next steps, to take flight, to accept that this chapter of my life was complete. The final quiz was in allowing others to help.

———

My time in the chrysalis was a sacred journey of transformation that could not have been different. I could not have learned the lessons or changed my life in any other way. I was carefully guided and watched over every moment.

During this remarkable time in my life, I was introduced, and came to know, many faces of the Divine. I met and conversed with angels, who welcomed me onto this strange path and guided my early steps. Power animals taught me new ways to see and understand the unseen world. I re-friended Jesus, who taught me to Love, to forgive, and to find joy. I felt the deeper, pervasive Presence of the Divine intertwine with my everyday life, with each breath. And finally, I came to know God as me too.

I also knew that my journey was not over—that really, it had only just begun. There was ever so much more to learn and to transform within my still very imperfect self. This beautiful moment was simply an end to one chapter in my life and the beginning of a new one yet to be written, yet to be lived.

It would be a chapter, I imagined, filled with flitting here and there in my butterfly body. Of living lightly, ungrounded, sipping nectar, finding joy. Integrating the lessons learned in the chrysalis while being out there exploring the big wide world. Only time would tell ...

Acknowledgments

First and foremost, I wish to express my eternal gratitude to Spirit for lovingly guiding me on this unusual journey, helping me find the courage to move past my fears, and firmly holding me accountable for my thoughts and actions.

Secondly, I am the luckiest person alive to have a sister like Sue. She opened many doors into the world of Spirit for me and was my anchor when the storms of life blew hardest, standing by me and my illogical choices without question.

I have great appreciation for all the teachers who showed up for me just when I was ready to learn their lessons. For Connie, who opened my eyes to angels. For Archangel Michael and all the other angels who helped me discover that there was much more to me than I ever realized. And most especially my gratitude to Jesus, who healed my heart and showed me the path of love.

There were countless other teachers as well, who perhaps never saw themselves that way. Like the salespeople at my job, who taught me what hate feels like. The cashier at a grocery store whose genuine smile lifted my spirits on a very down day. Yes, I still remember you! Gratitude even to the gallery owner, the green tech company, and the scammers who dished out the hard lessons of humility, surrender, forgiveness, and acceptance.

Deep, deep gratitude for my dear friends Patty, Gay, Kay, and for all the others who loved me for who I was, encouraged me to keep "becoming" and appreciated the gifts and abilities I discovered along the way.

More recently, my gratitude goes out to Willow, for taking the time to read the first draft of this story and offering her thoughtful feedback and encouragement.

Finally, my publisher Jennifer and her team at Bright Communications deserve a serious round of applause and gratitude for the great care, support, and respect they have given to help birth these words into book form. I'm so grateful, Jennifer, that our paths crossed long before I knew I needed you!

––––

A note from Kathy:

I hope you enjoyed *Chrysalis!* I'd love to hear from you! I am also available to speak and/or to offer art classes. Please inquire if interested. You can contact me via my website KathyFordauthor.com. If you'd like to see more of my art, please visit KathyFordartist.com

Peace!

Kathy

About the Author

Kathy Ford is an artist and author whose writing "career" began in elementary school when she submitted an essay to a writing contest about Earth Day (when Earth Day was brand new on the calendar). She was excited to win an award for the essay and received three tree seedlings as her prize. For many years, she proudly watched them grow into towering evergreens in her backyard.

She was a cable TV designer, systems analyst, maternity clothing store owner, business process re-engineering consultant, manager (and later VP) of customer service, demand planning, and logistics functions in various consumer products companies.Now retired, she continues to learn and try new things, including writing a book and training to become a yoga therapist. She still paints and shows her work in local galleries.

www.ingramcontent.com/pod-product-compliance
Lightning Source LLC
Chambersburg PA
CBHW051305120626
46547CB00015B/2103